WHO AM I?

Your Personal Journey
To Finding Peace

Elizabeth
Baker

A
JANET
THOMA
BOOK

THOMAS NELSON PUBLISHERS
Nashville

All of the characters in the stories are composites of people we met during the years of our ministry. Names, genders, and other identifying characteristics have been changed to protect the privacy of those people.

Unless otherwise noted, all Scripture quotations are from THE NEW KING JAMES VERSION of the Bible. Copyright © 1979, 1980, 1982, Thomas Nelson, Inc., Publishers.
Scripture quotations from the KING JAMES VERSION of the Bible are marked KJV throughout the text.
Scripture quotations noted NIV are from The Holy Bible: NEW INTERNATIONAL VERSION. Copyright © 1978 by the New York International Bible Society. Used by permission of Zondervan Bible Publishers.
Published in Nashville, Tennessee, by Janet Thoma Books, a division of Thomas Nelson, Inc., Publishers, and distributed in Canada by Word Communications, Ltd., Richmond, British Columbia, and in the United Kingdom by Word (UK), Ltd., Milton Keynes, England.

Library of Congress TK

Printed in the United States of America

1 2 3 4 5 6 – 98 97 96 95 94 93

I wish to express my appreciation to a few special people who were instrumental in bringing this book to life. Without their help the project would have been much more difficult.

Jo Ann Powell, whose helpful suggestions and feedback were a guide and an encouragement as the work came together in its final form.

Jan Tater, who continually challenged me to use more Scripture references and provided step by step feedback as the work progressed.

Wesley Baker, my son, who provided the graphics used in Chapter 4, gave me a new computer system to work the final script, and was always so very patient when I called him at work because I couldn't get the command prompts right.

Floyd Elliott, my boss at CCR Counseling, who provided his encouragement and challenge both for this book and my life.

Chris Wommack, for permission to use his song "We Have Been Accepted."

Cindy Bailey, for permission to use her poem "Glass Wall."

CONTENTS

PART ONE

How Did I Lose Myself?

CHAPTER 1 ✌

Symptoms of a Lost Self

I remember the first time I became aware of that empty, isolating fog. I was almost thirty. There had come a rare snow to Texas, and I was standing by the kitchen window watching my three children play with their daddy around a newly made snowman. I could hear them laugh, but it left my heart strangely numb. It was not that my heart was sad, it was just cold.

I stood there and tried to remember the last time I had laughed. I couldn't recall. Oh, there had been times when my throat gave out the sounds called laughter, and times when I could feel my face grin. But it was all surface. Inside, nothing was touched. Nothing was alive. I had lost my sense of identity. Somewhere in the daily rush, self had died.

I wasn't sure when it had happened. The deadness had crept into my life like a mist. Slowly, quietly, it settled over me.

At the time I thought it strange that I could not pinpoint the day the fog rolled in. But now as a professional counselor, I know that most of us who experience this phenomenon are not sure when the mist came or even when we first noticed it. There is just a moment when we wake up and realize a fog has moved in and self has been swallowed up and disappeared.

There are many words in vogue these days used to describe the phenomenon of a lost self. Sometimes we call it an identity crisis, or we may say we feel empty, searching, agitated, or alone.

We may feel we don't belong or that deep inside we are not alive anymore.

Some may wonder if they are having a midlife crisis, and others suspect we are just plain going crazy. But a lost sense of self seldom has anything to do with true psychological pathology. There is no pill to cure it. And though feelings such as those described above may be a part of various psychiatric disorders, the feelings themselves do not mean a person is "going crazy." Seeing a counselor or pastor may help if someone is caught in that difficult to describe fog, but most often the hurting individual is both sane and normal.

Below you will find some statements that others have used to describe this separated, lost feeling. Check those boxes that most nearly describe how you currently feel. As you work, remember, THIS IS NOT A TEST. There are no right or wrong answers. You will not receive a grade, and you are not being judged. There is no rule that says you can't change your mind or erase something or make qualifying notes by your check marks. The ONLY purpose for this exercise and all those that follow is that of self discovery.

1. ☐ I often feel like an actor performing my life rather than living it.

2. ☐ I know in my head that God forgives me, but I have never felt clean deep inside.

3. ☐ I believe that I am very different from other people.

4. ☐ When I am in a mall or another public place, I like to study the people around me, but I don't think of myself as one of them.

5. ☐ I am very comfortable teaching or giving advice or leading, but I am uncomfortable relating to people as peers.

6. ☐ I cry or laugh easily, but it feels shallow and unreal.

7. ☐ I feel OK as long as I am serving or complimenting others but find it very difficult when others are serving or complimenting me.

8. ☐ I am confused inside and don't know what I want from life anymore.

9. ☐ I have continual doubts about my salvation and acceptance by God.

10. ☐ I feel distant from God, and He has never comforted me as He has others.

11. ☐ I am lonely even in a crowd.

12. ☐ The only reason my friends stay around me is for what I can do for them.

13. ☐ I believe God will have to do a special job on me because my sins are different from or worse than those of other people.

14. ☐ I cry for no reason.

15. ☐ I explode for no reason.

THE FEELINGS

I suppose if there is one word to best describe the phenomenon I want to address, it would be "disconnected." A lost sense of self creates a drifting feeling that is instantly identifiable to anyone who has been there. It is a feeling of life going on day after day as it always has, but we don't seem to connect with the flow.

The loss of self can create an isolation that is so intense it is almost palpable. We move through the days like robots performing in a bad play that someone else has written. Cindy Bailey was able to express her feelings about being isolated from others through poetry.

Glass Wall

Surrounded by a glass wall
Seen only by myself
This cool exterior protects me,
Keeps me safe.
Holds the world at a distance
That I might observe it,
Yet not experience the pain
Of its vulnerability.

Surrounded by a glass wall
Seen only by myself.
Your words I hear plainly, clearly;
The wall does not drown them out.
Inside this wall I'm screaming,
But it is lost and unheard,
Reverberating within my little glass world.

Surrounded by a glass wall
Seen only by myself.
Clenching my fist in desperation,
I reach out to pound on the wall with my fist.
Ask for help, reach out—
But I resist;
Terrified by the sound of breaking glass.

I sometimes use Cindy's poem in therapy sessions. I will ask someone to read it and then ask them to tell me about a time when they felt the wall between themselves and others. Below, write about your own response to the idea of glass walls.

_____

_____

_____

_____

_____

We build walls to protect ourselves from pain. Our basic temperament and family background determine the method we will use in the construction process.

1. Charlene is the life of every party. The attention is always on her as she gives out a steady stream of chatter. Many people think they know Charlene, but in truth, few if any people know her. Charlene uses the high energy stream of words to turn attention away from her real feelings. She is hiding behind words.

2. Deborah has developed vanishing into a fine art. She smiles pleasantly, but seldom speaks. She is easily overlooked, almost fading into the woodwork if there is a crowd. She is always on the outside looking in and would panic if drawn into the center of attention.

3. Beth has always been large, but she gained an additional fifty pounds about ten years ago when she went through a divorce. She has lost the weight twice since then, but both times her anxiety level got so high she was put on medication to control the panic. Beth can relate well and be somewhat relaxed around others as long as she has her pounds to keep people away and hide her sexuality.

4. Jennifer is a classic workaholic. She is constantly involved in one project after another and has little time for relationships. She avoids her husband. Sex died years ago. She feels inadequate with the children, and although she buys them toys and proudly has their picture made, she seldom really relates to them and prefers to let someone else do the disciplining. Jennifer will give her family anything . . . except her heart.

5. Joan leads a double life. Part of her shows up at work each day and even goes to church a few times each year. But a separate and very large part of her has a cocaine addiction. Her husband has caught on and is threatening to take the kids and leave but even he has no idea of how bad things are. Cocaine is both Joan's master and her hiding place. She can take a hit of coke and check out of life for at least a little while. She can disconnect from painful emotions and the bills and the responsibilities of a family. She can literally make the world go away.

6. Carol has a mouth like acid. She will always find a reason why someone is unworthy or in need of correction. From her bitter, critical viewpoint, every church she has ever been a part of has disappointed her and failed to measure up to God's expectations, every friend has wronged her grievously, every family member is alienated from her, no one in her life has understood her, everyone has always betrayed her.

These are only a few of the many different methods humans have used to build walls. Charlene with her wall of continual talking, Deborah with her wall of shyness, Beth with her wall of fat, Jennifer with her wall of work, Joan with her wall of addiction, and Carol with her wall of bitter criticism, have all found favored ways to retreat from others, self, and God.

SEARCH FOR THE "NEW" YOU

When the walls go up, the fog settles in. We lose ourselves inside that tiny glass world of walls, and the emptiness inside drives us to try and find a way back to life again.

One solution that is often tried is to search for a new person to replace the empty one we have become. It is no wonder that we seek for this "new" person because the news media has been pounding us with the idea for years.

Just take a look at the supermarket tabloids. They continually tantalize us with promises of transforming us into a "new" person. They claim that this diet, that fashion, leaving home to get a job, having a full makeover, having an affair, or going to a spa will solve our problems and make us "new." And, when we are made new we will be in very good company. I have been invited to meet the "new" Liz Taylor a dozen or more times. Even Princess Di has been announced as "new" three times that I can count. But the problem with this tabloid solution is that it doesn't work.

Many women have tried to find themselves by rearranging the present. Some go so far as to change life-styles completely in a frantic effort to live authentically and achieve a sense of identity: A new diet, changing marriage partners, running away from home, having an affair, switching careers, changing churches, buying a sports car. All have been tried. And, all have been unsuccessful.

It is easy to understand why the tabloids are making money with this marketing tool. It hurts to be locked alone in a glass bubble and lost in a fog, and it is logical to assume that a "new" self will fix our problem and set us free.

But the truth is that we have only one self and no matter how much new we put on the outside, the core of isolation will follow us.

THREE AREAS OF SEPARATION

When we lose our sense of self, we lose the connector that would have linked us to at least three vital relationships: Personal emotions, others, and God. If we want to become alive again, we will have to risk the pain of examining and reconnecting life to these three areas.

Go back over the statements in the exercise on page 4 and give each a number from 0 to 5 depending on how strongly you feel that statement accurately describes where you are now. Jot those numbers in the margins of that exercise by each check mark before you continue reading.

Statements 1, 6, 8, 14, and 15 correspond to our separateness from self. Statements 3, 4, 5, 7, and 12 correspond to a separateness from others; and statements 2, 9, 10, 11, and 13 correspond to our separateness from God and His cleansing from sin.

Record your scores below, placing the number you gave each statement in the blank spaces next to the numbers and then adding the scores.

Separate from self:	Separate from others:	Separate from God:
1. ⬚	3. ⬚	2. ⬚
6. ⬚	4. ⬚	9. ⬚
8. ⬚	5. ⬚	10. ⬚
14. ⬚	7. ⬚	11. ⬚
15. ⬚	12. ⬚	13. ⬚
⬚ Total	⬚ Total	⬚ Total

Which area did you score highest in? Do your scores reflect how you feel? If not, in which area do you believe you are the most disconnected and alone?

Separated from Personal Emotions

When we lose our identity, we also strangely become lost from ourselves. A gulf that we cannot bridge separates our emotions from the reality around us. Emotions may pop up and vanish or sit silently for years and smolder without names. We don't know why they come or why they go. We can even become isolated from our own bodies. We look in a mirror and a stranger looks back.

Inside our cold, glass bubbles we vacillate between intently feeling about tiny matters and total numbness. We may completely "lose it" when someone cuts in front of us in traffic and flood the aisle with tears during a movie but feel little or nothing during times of crisis or family joy.

Perhaps you have experienced the strangeness of your head and your heart traveling in two different worlds. Have there been times your emotions didn't seem to match the circumstances in the outside world? Write about one below.

_____

_____

_____

_____

_____

Separated from God

When we lose ourselves, we also lose our connection with God. We still know He is up there. Somewhere. Maybe.

But, whatever the case, we know we can't seem to reach Him anymore. There is no sense of being forgiven and maybe even no sense of needing forgiveness. His presence is lost in the mist. We hear others talk about how they feel Him near or how they get answers to their prayers, but we are different, isolated, alone.

We are also isolated from the Christian family even though we may still attend services each week. We sit in the congregation and we are alone. And although our American culture and many of our church denominations encourage us never to get more intimate with our Christian brothers and sisters than to look at the back of their neck on Sunday morning, something in us tells us there ought to be more. But we know that "more" is not part of our spiritual experience.

When we have lost our identity, we often feel as though we have lost God. We sympathize with David when he cried, "My God, My God, why have You forsaken Me? / Why are You so far from helping Me, / And from the words of My groaning? / O My God, I cry in the daytime, but You do not hear; / And in the night season, and am not silent" (Ps. 22:1–2).

If you have experienced feelings of separation from God, write about it below. He is the Lord God Almighty, and it is not a good idea to either shake our fist at Him or turn our back on Him; yet it is also true that we can't tell Him anything about our hearts that He doesn't already know. Honestly saying what we feel will not surprise or upset Him, and it can be the first step in our healing.

Separated from Others

When we do not know our selves and cannot find our God, how can we expect to connect with others? We feel that something about us is wrong and needs to be hidden. We don't connect on an honest, comfortable level with others because we are frightened of the pain that might occur if we were rejected by them. We can't risk exposure, so we put on a plastic front and the circle of isolation becomes complete as we retreat within our world of glass walls.

S H A M E

The force that drives us to retreat behind walls is most often shame. We are embarrassed. We don't want to risk exposure to others or God and we don't want to face emotions that we may find unpleasant. We make a judgment on ourselves, and we don't like the verdict. This verdict has been based on two sources of evidence.

The first source of evidence is from the outside. Someone tells us by word or deed that we are bad or lacking or less than adequate. When we believe this external judgment and internalize it, a feeling of shame will result.

The second source of evidence comes entirely from inside. We set up a standard of what "should" and "ought" to be. We hear this internal source in the private conversations that go on in our heads as we talk with ourselves continually through the day. When phrases like "You are so stupid," "They are laughing at you," "You should have known better" continually dance around in our mind, the poison of shame will slowly force us back into an isolated shell and the fog will quickly follow.

THE WAY HOME

Remember the old Dobie Gillis show from the 1960s? Its central characters were Dobie—a clean-cut, girl crazy adolescent—and his sidekick, Maynard. Maynard was what we called at the time a "beatnik." Complete with beads, sandaled feet, and goatee, he was a comical character who avoided work at all cost and was not noted for his intelligence.

One day Maynard informed Dobie that he would soon be leaving on a long trip. Many real life rock stars of that time were making pilgrimages to the Far East to consult with gurus about the meaning of life. Maynard had decided that he, too, needed to go to a mountain in Tibet to search for himself. There on the mountain he would speak with the ancient wise men and find out who he really was.

Dobie replied with candor, "Maynard, you will never find yourself on a mountain in Tibet." "Why not?" asked his friend. "Because you didn't lose yourself on a mountain in Tibet," the teenage sage replied.

I always get a little uneasy when Hollywood says something profound, but occasionally accidents do happen. It is biblically and psychologically true: We will never find ourselves by searching for a new self out there somewhere. There is no "new" us on a mountain in Tibet.

God does have a solution for the phenomenon of fog and walls and a lost, drifting self, but it will not be found by searching outside ourselves. It is found by searching within. We must know ourselves and accept ourselves, then, once we have a firm hold on who we are, we give ourselves away to Him. When that happens, the fog will lift, the walls will come down, and we will be free.

This guidebook is designed to lead you through that inward search. We will examine your body, your memories, your will, and your mind. The book is divided into six parts. This first part is a look at the dynamics of how we lost ourselves. Parts two, three, and four are an autobiographical search of your genetics, environment, and decisions. In part five we will look at ourselves as God sees us, and in part six we will work on an in-depth emotional acceptance of all we have found.

At the end of each chapter you will find a series of thought questions and a blank page for your own personal summation. This is more than a blank page for miscellaneous notes. It is a stepping-stone to record your own personal journey. To receive maximum benefit from your work it is important that you spend a little time thinking about each step and writing down what you feel.

Some questions you might consider are: Why did you buy this book? What do you hope to change? Do you feel disconnected from life? How big a role has shame played in your past? Do you have a history of being abused? Which exercise created the biggest emotional impact on you? Why do you think that particular one touched you? How would your life be different if you had a strong identity structure and good self-esteem?

Personal Summation:

❧ CHAPTER 2

Throwing Away the Pieces

It may surprise or even shock you, but I believe Christians in general are not self-centered enough. I know that idea shocked me the first time I was honest enough to admit it. The whole idea sounded so prideful!

But before you judge my attitude as non-biblical, please understand what I mean by "self-centered." When I say Christians need to be more self-centered, I am not talking about being self-indulgent, selfish, preoccupied with self-defense, or giving ourselves permission to engage in self-destructive behaviors.

When I say "self-centered," I am talking of the need to clear enough time and emotional energy to take a long, honest appraisal of reality: Our personal reality. We stand alone in a white spotlight and shut our mouth long enough to quietly, thoughtfully consider what God created when He made us a unique individual with our special history, our feelings, and our thoughts. We look at all we are by birth and circumstance and consider the choices we have made and the effect these have had on who we are now.

This is a true centering on self, and I believe it is a necessary step in the process of spiritual growth, but it is also a scary step. Not many are willing to risk such self-examination.

I know for many years I was not willing to do that examination because I thought that consideration of self was something a

Christian must avoid at all cost. If I wanted to be Christlike, I had to run away from any thoughts about self. Self was to be forced so far into the background that it was almost non-existent. Self-forgetfulness was the goal I was to aim for, not self-awareness!

But after years of struggling to achieve peace and ministry through self-avoidance, I found that running away from my reality, refusing to admit my needs, fighting against the nature God gave me, avoiding emotional awareness, and turning my head each time a memory from the past came into consciousness did little to advance true spiritual growth. Time has shown that I was not alone in my misguided project of self-avoidance. Many of God's children work hard at avoiding a knowledge of self and think that what they are doing is being spiritual.

Below is a list of statements that have been taught by various churches and well intentioned families. Some of the statements about self have likely affected your life. Grade each statement by circling the appropriate response. As you work, remember that if you heard a statement repeated often enough, it probably influences you on an emotional level even though you may fight it on a logical level.

1. People who express personal wants and desires are selfish.

Strongly agree   *(Agree)*   *No opinion*   *Disagree*   *Strongly disagree*

2. "I" is the center of "sin" and is a word we should try to eliminate from our conversation.

Strongly agree   *Agree*   *No opinion*   *(Disagree)*   *Strongly disagree*

3. It is a prideful act to send someone a picture of yourself.

Strongly agree   *(Agree)*   *No opinion*   *Disagree*   *Strongly disagree*

4. When someone gives you a compliment, it is wrong to feel good and/or mentally agree with the statement.

Strongly agree   *(Agree)*   *No opinion*   *Disagree*   *Strongly disagree*

5. It is not Christlike to admit you have done a good job or excelled in some way.

Strongly agree　　*(Agree)*　　*No opinion*　　*Disagree*　　*Strongly disagree*

6. Pride in all forms is always wrong.

Strongly agree　　*(Agree)*　　*No opinion*　　*Disagree*　　*Strongly disagree*

7. A good motto to live by is: I will always consider God first, others second, and myself last.

Strongly agree　　*(Agree)*　　*No opinion*　　*Disagree*　　*Strongly disagree*

8. The Bible tells us to "take no thought" about ourselves.

Strongly agree　　*Agree*　　*(No opinion)*　　*Disagree*　　*Strongly disagree*

9. We should be careful not to compliment children too much, or they may think everything is OK and quit trying.

Strongly agree　　*Agree*　　*No opinion*　　*(Disagree)*　　*Strongly disagree*

10. If we occasionally daydream about people admiring us or of doing something special and being noticed, we are likely full of ungodly pride.

Strongly agree　　*(Agree)*　　*No opinion*　　*Disagree*　　*Strongly disagree*

I would encourage you to review your responses when you finish this chapter and see if any of your opinions have changed.

Sometimes the teaching we have received or even passed on to others is misleading. I find this especially true for those who come from a family background of abuse or neglect. They are very prone to use statements like those above to prove to themselves that they really are as worthless as they feel. If taken to extreme, teachings such as these give Christians a "holy" excuse for not examining the past or exposing what they really feel to others, themselves, or even to God.

Christians often try to be compassionate toward others but avoid personal feelings of sorrow. They want to live a life of forgiveness by never admitting to pain. Troubling memories are brushed under their mental rug. Personal needs are never acknowledged until the pressure of unmet needs makes them go off like a volcano spewing lava.

All this activity may look good on the outside and it can give the illusion of progress, but it most often does nothing more than sap spiritual energy. Remember: The wind going past your ears is not always a sign of progress being made. It can be a sign that you are falling.

Trying to live a Christian life while avoiding a knowledge of self is like trying to score a home run in baseball while avoiding first base.

Self-search is not an ego trip or a source of vanity because it is only after we have looked inside ourselves and come to some sort of peace about what we have found that we are in a position to minister to those outside. After we have passed this first step of growth, we can serve others without becoming a doormat, and we will be able to hold our dignity even in situations where we are not given respect by others.

THE FINAL AUTHORITY

The Bible is our final authority for determining whether any particular thing we do is a sin. It is the measuring stick by which all things are judged. And it will tell us whether or not self-examination is acceptable to God.

The following brief Bible study is designed to walk you through the scriptural principles of pride and self-examination. Look up the Bible references and mark your answers true or false. Remember, *this is not a test.* Feel free to make qualifying notes by your answers or mark both true and false if that seems right. You will find an answer key at the end of the chapter where I have given my responses and a brief explanation.

1. When Jesus' disciples gave Him the compliment of calling Him "Teacher" (master) and "Lord" (boss, owner, ruler), Jesus gave them an example of humility by playing down those comments (John 13:13).
   True   False

2. It is always right to boast (feel good about, comment favorably) about the Lord, but a person should never boast (feel good about, comment favorably) about their own ability (compare Ps. 34:2 and 2 Cor. 10:8).
   True   False

3. The Bible commands us to spend time examining ourselves and looking inward (1 Cor. 11:28).
   True   False

4. It is wrong for a person to feel good about being lifted up, exalted, or honored (Matt. 23:12; James 4:10; 1 Peter 5:6).
   True   False

5. Some of the writers of the Bible spent time thinking to themselves and carrying on a mental dialogue (Ps. 77:4–6).
   True   False

6. It is a waste of time to remember the past or spend effort to put it in the proper perspective (Deut. 5:15; Rev. 2:5).
   True   False

7. It shows a lack of faith to examine our belief system (2 Cor. 13:5).
   True   False

8. It is wrong to take pride in our work for the Lord (Gal. 6:4).
   True   False

9. It is OK to compare ourselves with others because competi-

tion spurs us on to greater work for the Lord (2 Cor. 10:12–13).
True   False

Home and church are usually the first place we learn what pride is and how much attention can be paid to personal needs and feelings. Hopefully, these teachings were in line with the Word of God, but for some of us they were not, and now as adults we need to go back and examine what we have learned. In the space below write about a specific memory where you were taught by example or word about the subject of self-consideration and pride.

_____

_____

_____

_____

_____

_____

_____

_____

How did this teaching make you feel?

_____

_____

_____

_____

Do you think it affected your feelings later in life?

_____

_____

_____

_____

Do you believe this teaching was consistent with Bible truth? Why or why not?

_____

_____

Identifying what is and is not pride can be a problem for the Christian who is in rebellion, but it can also be a problem for those with a tender conscience who have either been taught incorrectly or who have received good teaching through the filter of childhood abuse.

Below you will find a list of statements that indicate a sinful form of pride. Some may be a bit confusing until you read the rest of the chapter and understand why I believe they indicate pride. To complete this exercise, check those statements that remind you of yourself even if you have trouble thinking of them as prideful.

1. ☐ I frequently use the phrase, "I know what you are thinking..." when I am angry at someone.

2. ☐ When I walk into a room, I am instantly aware of the men (women) in the room and how they perceive me.

3. ☐ I frequently apologize for inconsequential things.

4. ☐ I am uncomfortable being seen as one of the crowd.

5. ☐ When I listen to a performer or speaker or preacher, I critique them to others around me.

6. ☐ I drop names.

7. ☐ I exaggerate when I tell personal stories or talk about my feelings.

8. ☐ When someone else is telling something positive about themselves, I feel compelled to humble them and bring them back down to earth.

9. ☐ When someone tells a personal story, I immediately follow with a bigger story about my life and accomplishments.

10. ☐ I depend on external things such as clothes, makeup, or car to make myself acceptable to others.

11. ☐ I frequently criticize those in authority.

12. ☐ I feel that people have been unfair to me most of my life.

THE TRAP OF PRIDE

Pride was listed by the ancient church as one of the seven deadly sins. Proverbs 13:10 warns us that ALL struggling among people and fighting is rooted in pride. When pride comes, shame and destruction are not far behind (Prov. 11:2; Prov. 16:18). Jesus listed pride right along with murder, adultery, theft, and lewdness, and God says that He hates pride and arrogance (Prov. 8:13).

If we accept the Word of God, we have no trouble believing that pride is wrong, but we may have a lot of trouble defining exactly what pride is and what it is not.

In our Americanized English when we see someone who does not take care of themselves or their possessions, we say "they have no pride." Is it pride to treat ourselves and our belongings well? Does the word proud always indicate sin? Thinking back on my rural heritage, it was common to ask an older person how they were doing and have them respond, "Oh, I am doin' real proud," meaning that they felt healthy and things were going well.

When struggling with the question of pride, it has helped me to differentiate between the good feelings connected with reaching a standard and the wrong use of a split standard when judging. Feeling joy because we reach a goal set for ourselves is godly pride, but using one standard for ourselves and a different standard for others is sinful pride.

When I excuse or rationalize away my errors but hold my neighbor responsible for every minor mistake, I have put myself above him unjustly and I am guilty of sinful pride. That double standard is what most of us normally think of as the sin of pride.

But there is another double standard that is not so quickly recognized, yet it is just as sinful and just as much ungodly pride. Christians sometimes make the mistake of calling this pride "holy." This form of pride is the double standard where I put myself below everyone else. If I hold myself accountable and beat myself without mercy each time I fall short of the standard while I excuse others for the same error, I am still guilty of pride because I am still using a split standard. This false humility is nothing more than the same old pride, only in this case it's running in reverse gear.

This condemning of self is pride because every time I hit myself with an "I should have" statement, I indicate that I believe I "could" have done it if I had only tried harder. Deep down, we think that the ability is in self, or we would not be beating self for failure.

We would never tell a man without legs that he should walk because we recognize the obvious truth that the ability is just not there, but we tell ourselves that we should have been perfect and never blink at the incredulity of that absurd statement.

It is one thing to repent and/or accept our responsibility for an issue, but it is quite another to punish ourselves for oversights, honest mistakes, being human, and—that most common but most absurd—failure to make everyone around us happy all the time.

We often criticize and punish ourselves for not meeting these impossible and absurd goals, and unfortunately, we sometimes identify this self-punishment as humility.

Paul talked about those who used a standard of humility that looked good on the outside but did nothing to constrain sinful indulgences (Col. 2:23). This was a false humility of self-effort that made a show of harsh treatment for self, and although it had the appearance of wisdom, it was full of regulations and lacked real value.

Godly pride is a rejoicing in the soul over a job well done or a lesson of character learned. This kind of pride may notice the difference between self and others and may even recognize that the conduct of self is more righteous than the conduct of another, and that creates another problem with pride. How can I know I am better than someone else without being prideful?

HOLIER THAN THOU?

I remember my teenage daughter's shyness when she approached me. She was the firstborn, a gentle soul who would rather give in than fight. Her tender conscience was often causing her unnecessary trouble and this time seemed no different.

"Mama," she tentatively began while looking at the floor, "how do you keep from feeling holier than thou when . . . well . . . you know."

"When you really are more holy than someone else?" I asked, finishing her sentence for her.

The problem had come about at school when others called her names and accused her of pride because she did not engage in the same activities as many of her peers.

The answer to that dilemma is found not in the split standard, but it is a question of who sets the standard. Is it me against them? My standards against their standards? If so, we have become unwise and are close to the sin of pride. But if we are using the standard God set and judging both self and others, then we are on safe ground.

There is no doubt about it. A true believer is more holy than a hypocrite. An honest man is better than a thief. Someone who drinks and curses and fails to support their family is wrong and someone who is temperate, loving, and faithful to work as they can is right.

We do not have to sit in judgment on someone who is caught in a lie; we simply agree with the judgment that God has already passed. Lying is wrong, and we are free to say so without being proud or judgmental.

However, there are two cautions we need to remember when we begin this observational judging. First, we can only see the outside results, not the motive. And second, we must make sure that it is God's standard we are using, not our own personal preferences.

We have limited access to the heart. In fact, it might be more accurate to say that we have none. We can only judge the outside, the behavior. We are almost always on dangerous ground when we say "I know what you think" or "I know why you did that." Only God knows someone's intent and purpose. We can only say, "By your behavior you appear to believe."

Sometimes we attempt to judge where God has made no clear direction in His Word. In a situation like this we often want to insist that others meet our standards, and we refuse to give them the freedom to be themselves. We try to do God's job for Him and set standards where none exist. This it totally off limits for God's child, and besides that, it makes others mad real quick!

GOD'S GIFT

In a very practical sense our personal self is the greatest gift God has given us. This gift of self involves all our physical attributes, personal history, and freedom. It is our mind and our body and our spiritual ears that have the capacity to hear and know Him.

One way to visualize this concept is to imagine that God has sent us a big box by special messenger. We hear a knock at the door and answer to find the box sitting on the step. The box has a big tag on it reading, "Fragile, box contains one human. Handle with care and upon completion, return to sender." Signed, "Heaven's Shipping House, Sincerely, God."

It would be an insult to our Creator to turn our eyes away and fail to examine everything He gave us when He sent that box.

The Bible says that we will learn about God by studying His creation (Rom. 1:20). There will never be another fragment of creation we can observe as closely as our own heart; there will be no history we will have as much insight to as our own; we will never see grace as close up as we can observe it in action on our own shame. What a pity to let this opportunity for learning go by as we disregard God's gift!

However, we must be aware of certain dangers as we examine our gift, and perhaps it is because of these dangers that so much teaching has discouraged people from opening their box and examining with delight their gift of self. One trap is pride, which we have already discussed, and the other is its close cousin: Measurement.

THE TRAP OF MEASUREMENT

All measurement is a comparison. We might compare the length of a pencil to a ruler or the heat of the day to how high the mercury rises on a scale; we can only measure one thing as we compare it to another thing.

The Bible gives us a whole bag of measuring devices to be used for various purposes. For instance, the Law is a balance scale we can use to measure what is good and what is bad. The Sermon on the Mount is a yardstick for determining how our daily living measures up to God's expectations. Calvary measures the horror of sin; resurrection measures the power of God.

But there is one measuring stick that we are strongly warned *never* to use. Of course, that is the first one we want to grab. We have a strong inclination to measure ourselves against each other.

As we unwrap our gift box from God and begin a delightful search to find and accept all it contains, we have a tendency to look down the street at all the other people standing on their front porches unwrapping similar boxes from God.

We notice that the man next door got more talent. Sister Sue got more money. Aunt Sophie got a great body. And we heard that a man named John who lives on the next block got a life where God answers all his prayers instantly, and he never was sick a day in his life, and he will appear on TV next week to tell everyone about how they can get a life like that too!

All this observation of others is not sin; the sin only comes when we look back at our own box and start to measure ourselves or God's fairness by how our box stacks up against others'. If we compare and come out with what we believe is less than others, we are embarrassed and we begin to question God. If we compare and come out with what we think is more than others, we view it as His special attention to us or proof of our personal worth, thus setting ourselves slightly above most of our neighbors.

Paul warned us about comparison in Galatians 6:4–5 when he states: "Each one should test his own actions. Then he can take pride in himself, without comparing himself to somebody else, for each one should carry his own load" (NIV).

A few years later in another letter, when Paul's own worth and ability were brought into question, he replied, "For we dare not class ourselves or compare ourselves with those who commend themselves. But they, measuring themselves by themselves, and comparing themselves among themselves, are not wise. We, however, will not boast beyond measure, but within the limits of the sphere which God appointed us" (2 Cor. 10:12–13).

If we want to be wise and happy as we unwrap and examine our heavenly gift, we had best keep our hands off the measuring stick of comparison.

As long as we leave the measurement of others up to God, we will never be in any danger of sinning. When we engage in an honest search for the self we feel we have lost, we will become better and stronger servants, not selfish egotists.

OUR EXAMPLE: JESUS

One of the clearest examples of how knowledge of self-worth and true humility work together for the service of others is given in John 13:3–5.

John begins this story by talking about Jesus' knowledge of Himself: "Jesus, knowing that the Father had given all things into His hands, and that He had come from God and was going to God, rose from supper and laid aside His garments, took a towel and girded Himself . . . and began to wash the disciples' feet."

Knowledge of who He was and an awareness of personal worth was the springboard for service. Jesus did not avoid compliments, run from knowledge of Himself, pretend that He was less than what He knew Himself to be, or apologize for the truth about Himself. Rather, it was this secure knowledge of His personal worth and dignity that made service so noble as others looked at His example. It was this knowledge that made it possible for Him to perform without self-deprecation.

SELF-EVALUATION

Self-evaluation is not pride. Even when that evaluation has an element of rejoicing, it is not sin and is nowhere discouraged by the Lord.

Self-examination was encouraged by Paul. We are to examine everything about ourselves (1 Cor. 11:28) and to pass judgment on what we find (v. 31). We are to check out our actions and feelings and see how these confirm or deny our faith (2 Cor. 13:5). The psalmist Asaph remarked that he meditated and inquired with himself about himself, his history, and his God (Ps. 77:5–6) and how all these fit together. Both Jews and Christians are told to remember their past and consider it (Deut. 5:15; Rev. 2:5). It is not necessary to avoid knowledge of self and the influences that have molded us into what we are in order to be spiritual. In fact, avoiding such knowledge will make spiritual growth more difficult.

We are told that we can learn about God by examining the creation God has made (Ps. 19:1), and there is no reason to assume that this consideration should exclude the examination of the creation of self.

The human experience is different from that of animal or

vegetable or angel or demon, and if we don't include self in our consideration of creation, we have left out a major part that is unlike all else. We are unique in our ability of conscience to know both good and evil (Gen. 3:22). This is the problem that awakens shame when we know we are less than what we should be. And we are unique as we participate in redemption and Jesus pays the price to take our shame away.

I remember an old hymn that we sang in the church where I grew up. One line was: "But when I sing redemption's story, They shall fold their wings. For angels never knew the joy that my salvation brings."

What a wonderful and mysterious gift God has given when He gave us our self. I hope and pray that you will find this book of self-exploration to be a joyful adventure, not a doubtful experience that we suspect a "good" Christian would never undertake!

It is my prayer and expectation that this book will make you more like the Master, not less, and that servanthood will become easier and have a new freedom that is not marred by the bondage of false humility that too often marks a Christian's work.

Complete this section by writing a summation of all you have learned thus far. Some questions you might consider: How comfortable am I with feeling godly pride in what I do and who I am? Has my service to others been from a volunteer position of strength or from the angle of a doormat? Did I learn any new information or gain any new insights about the Bible definition of pride? How do I feel about using this book?

Personal Summation:

A N S W E R   K E Y

The following are the answers for the exercise on page 20.

1. False. Jesus accepted their compliments because they were true.

2. False. Paul rejoiced in the abilities God had given him, and did not avoid talking about his joy.

3. True.

4. False. If God exalts or honors someone, failure to accept or be happy about that honor would be a dishonor to God.

5. True. Asaph (the writer of Psalm 77), David, and Solomon are only a few of those who spent time considering themselves, their past, and their feelings.

6. False. Both Old Testament Jews and Christians are commanded to remember their past.

7. False. Christian faith stands up well to honest scrutiny. There is no question we should be afraid to tackle with faith and honesty.

8. False. We are encouraged to take godly pride without comparison.

9. False.

CHAPTER 3 ❧

Does God Want Me to Search for Myself?

In the original story of Hansel and Gretel, the children were led deep into the woods by a wicked stepmother. The first time she led them in, Hansel overheard her plot and stuffed his pockets full of small white stones. He dropped these one by one along the trail as he and Gretel were led deeper and deeper into the dark woods. When they were finally abandoned, he led his sister back to the loving arms of their father and the safety of home by picking up the small stones he had dropped.

Like Hansel walking through the woods casting stones by the trail, we have walked the years of our lives casting off pieces of our self. Hansel intended to go back and pick up his stones, but we threw away tiny pieces of self planning never to see them again. We have hidden, ignored, denied, and fought against things that we did not want as part of our reality, and in the process we lost our sense of being.

We call this casting off self-rejection. It is a war between our soul and our reality. This rejection is not the times we changed things that were in our power but the times when we fought and kicked against the inevitable. It is our refusal to bend to reality and accept those things we cannot change.

The things we rejected and threw by the trail are as varied as life itself. The item may have been as small as a nickname that embarrassed us and we tried hard to forget, or as significant as a baby we decided to abort. It might have been a family secret or a background filled with poverty, our race, or our first marriage.

If we find ourselves living in a world of fog and glass walls, without a sense of self, purpose, or direction, it is very probable that we have cast hundreds of pieces of self by the trail, and at times the rejection that seemed the most inconsequential can become a turning point of life.

JENNY'S "TRUTH"

When Jenny was ten she took a lot of teasing about her name. They called her "Skinny Jenny," and she learned to hate the sound of those words. The cutting edge in the voices of her classmates let her know that "skinny" was bad.

Being young and impressionable, Jenny agreed with the judgment of her peers. She had little support from home telling her that her body was not embarrassing or bad, and she lacked the maturity to trust her own judgment as she looked in the mirror and saw the pretty blonde girl looking back. If her friends said she was damaged because of this thing called "skinny" that rhymed with her name, then it must be true.

Responding to that "truth" Jenny became shy and hid her body beneath loose-fitting clothes that were several sizes too big. And because "Jenny" was connected with "skinny," she would often take pretend names or say she was going to change her name when she grew up.

If this had been the extent of Jenny's experience, or if she had other evidence, such as a supportive father who told her what a special and pretty girl she was, Jenny would have been able to put her body and her name in proper perspective. She would have experienced embarrassment at the remarks of her classmates, gone through a time of questioning and adjustment, then emerged a stronger individual. But for Jenny, this was not to be.

Jenny's embarrassment grew to be shame. She learned to hate her body and her name. Over the years she developed an eating disorder as she became obsessed with having the "right" kind of body. For Jenny, that meant she had to be a size seven and weigh not more than one hundred and ten pounds no matter if it took throwing up five times a day to achieve that goal. By the time she was in high school, she had shortened her name and changed the spelling, calling herself Gin. After she finished her education, she preferred to be called Dr. Warring.

Of course, there were many factors involved in the development of Jenny Warring's life. The nicknames were not the only influence in Jenny Warring's forty-three years of development. But it is also true that at the tender age of ten, "Skinny Jenny" reacted to the pain of the shame she felt for having a "bad" body and a "dumb" name and fought against those realities with self-rejection.

At ten, Jenny lacked the maturity to examine the judgment she received from others. She only knew it hurt. In an effort to get rid of the hurt, Jenny tried to change the unchangeable (her body) and cut truth (her name) out of her life. Like Hansel dropping stones by the path, she tried to throw away those parts of her that created the pain, and by doing so, she threw away herself.

Many people experiment with name changes. Our name is a vital part of our identity. It says a lot about who we are and who we want to be. Name changing and nicknames can be part of the phases we all pass through as we develop, but at times our name can be a significant indication of how well we accept ourselves and how we want to be perceived by others.

Below, list your name in full using the spelling and order that are on your birth certificate. Then list those names that you have accepted or even requested as your own. For now, only include those names you wanted to be called. We will discuss painful nicknames in a later exercise.

The full name given me at birth was:

_____

Other names, titles, and nicknames that I have requested or
enjoyed are:

1. _____ 5. _____
2. _____ 6. _____
3. _____ 7. _____
4. _____ 8. _____

REJECTION:
AN ACTIVE WAR

The name changes that Jenny Warring experienced were more
than natural development and experimentation. They were an
unconscious effort to get away from who she perceived herself to
be. They were symbolic of a self-rejection which permeated her
life and personality.

Self-rejection is the internal force that pushes against life and
tries desperately to manipulate reality. It is an emotional back-
lash to shame that tries to force life into being pleasant again. It
is a war.

Self-rejection begins with the process of judgment. Because of
a judgment, we decide that something about ourselves is wrong
or bad, and it needs to be hidden. When the evidence outside
ourselves says we are less than adequate, or we conclude on the
basis of our own expectations that we are not what we "should"
be, shame wakes up inside us and we feel pain. We instinctively
want to get rid of the pain and set our world right again, but
because this "bad" thing is a part of us we end up caught in a
no-win situation. We want to get rid of or hide a bad thing so the
pain of shame will stop, but by throwing out the "bad" part, we
throw away a part of ourselves.

The cycle of judgment-shame-rejection-isolation is a process
that is as deeply ingrained in our being as the sin nature. It could
even be debated that they are one and the same. This cycle
penetrates our lives, our relationships, and our self-image. It

colors our thinking, shapes our behavior, and determines our ability to give and receive love.

The cycle begins with judgment, and often that judgment is based on false information and misunderstandings. At the age of ten Jenny began to let others tell her what was good and bad about herself, and she continued to follow this pattern through most of her adult life. Jenny always judged herself by what others said or what she thought others wanted.

We are surrounded by systems that tell us who we are and where we fit in the social structure. The school system, the family system, the church system, our work environment, and many other systems are continually giving us feedback about ourselves and others' perceptions of us. That is not necessarily bad. The problems come when we value their opinion more than we value what God says about us or when one of the systems breaks down, giving us only negative information.

Jenny lacked a feedback system that would have enabled her to properly balance the negative, external judgments being made by her schoolmates with other stronger, positive truth.

Some of the feedback systems that have been a part of your life are listed below. These systems will either have been supportive, neutral, or destructive in your life. Grade these systems on a scale from -2 to $+2$ indicating if each system has been very destructive (-2), neutral (0), or very supportive ($+2$). You may also want to add a name if your response applies only to one person in a system rather than the system itself.

1. Grade school teachers (name_____)
     -2 -1 0 $+1$ $+2$

2. Your church doctrine
     -2 -1 0 $+1$ $+2$

3. Older siblings (name _____)
     -2 -1 0 $+1$ $+2$

4. High school classmates (name _____)
   -2   -1   0   +1   +2

5. Girls when you were in middle school (name _____
   _____)
   -2   -1   0   +1   +2

6. Boys when you were in middle school (name _____
   _____)
   -2   -1   0   +1   +2

7. Your mother
   -2   -1   0   +1   +2

8. Your father
   -2   -1   0   +1   +2

9. Younger siblings (name _____)
   -2   -1   0   +1   +2

10. Sports participation
    -2   -1   0   +1   +2

11. Academics
    -2   -1   0   +1   +2

12. Extended family (name _____)
    -2   -1   0   +1   +2

13. The person you hung around most in high school
    (name _____)
    -2   -1   0   +1   +2

14. Your first boyfriend (name _____)
    -2   -1   0   +1   +2

15. (name _____)
   -2 -1 0 $+1$ $+2$

16. (name _____)
   -2 -1 0 $+1$ $+2$

17. (name _____)
   -2 -1 0 $+1$ $+2$

18. (name _____)
   -2 -1 0 $+1$ $+2$

THREE WAYS OF WAGING WAR

We combine statements we hear from our feedback systems with our own reasoning to form judgments about ourselves. At that moment we enter the judgment-shame-rejection-isolation cycle. This cycle is a war of the mind against reality.

The human mind is a marvelous instrument, and it tries very hard to do what our will tells it to do. If something about self is causing pain, and we don't want that thing around, the will sets itself to resist, and the mind does its best to cooperate and make the unwanted thing go away. Psychologists have named two of the ways our mind wages war as Repression and Suppression. But, with all due respect, I believe there is a third method of self-rejection and I have given it the scientific name of Stuck-in-the-muck.

All three of these methods will work because they do reduce or hide the pain for a season, but all three are guaranteed to eventually fail and leave us empty shells because all three involve hiding and lying to ourselves, others, and God.

When using the method of stuck-in-the-muck, we try to avoid the reality of the situation by building the issue up larger than life. This makes the situation appear impossible and allows us to avoid our responsibility to accept, forgive, and get on with life.

When we practice the method of suppression, we hide the issue from other people and place it internally on a dusty shelf. We can recall the issue and think about it if we want; otherwise the mind will hold it in limbo indefinitely.

However, the best trick of all may be repression where our mind almost volunteers to take the issue and completely lock it away out of conscious thought so we do not have to deal with its existence at all.

It might help to think of the three ways of waging the war of rejection against our souls as three layers, each one sinking deeper into the recesses of the soul.

Layer One: Stuck-in-the-muck

This layer involves a conscious resistance that is given frequent verbal and mental repetition. The rejected thing is always on the top of the mind and the tip of the tongue.

Layer Two: Suppression

Here, the rejected thing is mostly hidden from others. We know it is there and we frequently are embarrassed by it, but we don't want others to know our secret. We become part jailer, trying to keep the secret in, and part dishonest salesman, trying to keep the world from knowing the truth.

Layer Three: Repression

Sometimes we can be so successful at suppressing unwanted knowledge that we push it clear out of our consciousness. We may have little or even no memory of the event or we may lose the feelings connected with the unwanted thing. Yet, current relationships, unexplained behaviors, or feelings that "come from nowhere" give evidence that deep inside rejection has taken root somewhere and it is growing.

STUCK-IN-THE-MUCK

When I met Julia she was well into her sixties, depressed, and bitter. Her chief complaint was that she felt "unreal."

Julia was not psychotic. She was connected with reality and more or less well functioning except for bouts of depression which caused her to go to bed for days and sulk.

After listening to Julia's history it was evident that she was bitter about many things, including her feet.

It seemed that Julia's big feet were a family joke. She was also teased in school about her "gunboat-size" shoes. As she sat in my office, her feet did not look grotesque or deformed. While not petite, her size ten shoes were reasonable for this tall woman. But to Julia they were horrible.

For sixty years she had hated her feet and hated everyone who noticed them. Yet, she loudly and repeatedly mentioned the pain they caused her to anyone who got close enough to listen. And her feet were only the beginning of her complaints.

Julia had spent her lifetime compiling a list of things that she hated about herself and her life. Some were physical, some financial, some relational, some spiritual. Using her mind like a broken record, Julia went over and over her list year after year. By the time she came to my office, her stuck-in-the-muck was well entrenched.

Although Julia was aware of this self-rejection, her sourness had become a way of life and she refused to let it go. She held on to bitterness and thus held on to depression with all the physical and emotional pain that went with such a life.

She did not hold on because she liked pain or desired to stay depressed, but each time she verbalized the pain or let her hurt and anger replay in her mind or repeated her long list to someone who would listen, she felt a tiny bit better—even justified—for a moment. But ONLY for a moment.

Stuck-in-the-muck can take several forms. It can cause some people, like Julia, to live in extreme bitterness and to feel compelled to tell others about their pain. But a different person will experience a compulsion to relive, repeat, and condemn entirely inside their own mind. Those on the outside never know the war that is raging on the inside.

Write about a specific time when you observed someone else get stuck-in-the-muck and relive, repeat, and expose things to you or to others.

_____

_____

_____

_____

Try to recall when you made a negative judgment about something in your life and ended up stuck-in-the-muck (this includes times of exposure to others and also times when the compulsion was locked only in your own mind). Write what you remember about this experience.

_____

_____

_____

_____

_____

_____

SUPPRESSION

Sheila also complained of feeling alienated from herself and the world. Depressed and alone, she cried when she read the poem about the glass wall. Yet, as we discussed her history and present situation, she did not volunteer a list of things she rejected about herself. In fact, she avoided all references to anything closely related to shame.

She would begin to talk about something that disturbed her but immediately followed it with an excuse, or she would verbally backtrack and contradict herself. Because she was very determined to have a world that was neatly wrapped, explainable, and without pain, Sheila did not see the self-rejection she had practiced since childhood.

One of her many points of self-rejection was the fact that she had chosen to quit high school and marry. Sheila's embarrassment over her lack of a diploma was much deeper than one might expect. She was ashamed of this and went to great lengths to hide the fact from others.

Barely three years after her marriage, Sheila's husband became her ex-husband, and her life began to unravel quickly. Forced to support herself, Sheila lied about her lack of a diploma on job application forms, not only because she needed a job and doubted they would hire her without a diploma but because she couldn't face the shame she felt about that old decision. Sheila could have easily obtained a GED by going to the adult education building and filling out a few forms. But the thought of running into someone there who knew her was unbearable.

Sheila not only lied on job forms, she lied to friends and fellow employees. In time, she even invented a ten-year school reunion to talk about.

Sheila lied to herself too. Whenever some event (such as attending the graduation of a friend's daughter) brought the past to her conscious memory, she would struggle and almost cry, then quickly change mental gears and force her lips into a smile. Fighting the tears, she would tell herself that it didn't matter and push the thoughts away. Suddenly, the bad feelings would go away. Nothing was wrong. She was perfect. There was no need for shame.

Sheila preferred to deal with painful things by suppressing them. Anything in life that hurt her or confused her or didn't fit her ideal was pushed away. She just pretended it didn't exist. Small things, big things, anything!

But no matter how hard she tried to keep her pretend life in balance, reality had a way of crashing in uninvited. One marriage after another hit the rocks. Panic disorder and intense internal pain that refused to let her go were realities that could not be pushed aside.

Unlike stuck-in-the-muck, we cannot directly observe suppression in other people. We can only recognize it in ourselves because by its very definition it is a silent, hidden thing.

Write about a specific memory of when you used suppression to avoid dealing with a painful part of your life.

_____
_____
_____
_____
_____
_____

REPRESSION

Roberta was different from Julia or Sheila. She had only come to therapy because others in her discipleship program thought she had a problem. She had two failed marriages behind her and now wanted to marry again. Roberta was quiet, disciplined, and reserved. She had been a Christian for fifteen years.

Roberta had a very active and successful career in which she was required to interact with many strangers and to sell herself as well as her product, but this interaction with strangers was as close as anyone ever got to Roberta's heart. She hated the part of her church's service where people hugged each other or shook hands. She was strangely plastic and always turned the conversation away from herself. Everyone knew Roberta, but no one knew Roberta.

Roberta was aware of this hollow spot inside, but she only came to therapy because her discipleship teacher convinced her that unless she dealt with whatever caused her to keep people at a distance, she had little chance of success in a new marriage.

In our first session Roberta described herself as a contented but empty shell. Casual acquaintances of Roberta looked at her from the outside and thought she was a young, successful, and alive individual. But she saw herself from the inside and knew she was an unfeeling corpse. Still, this numb condition felt natural to her; she wasn't even sure she wanted to feel again.

As we worked together, I could detect nothing in her current situation that had caused the problem. But as we discussed her past, she began to relate some horrible issues of physical abuse. These incidents were explained in a matter-of-fact style. There was no change in her expression, no sign of anger, no tears, no grief. Roberta could talk of being a six year old who was beaten with an electric cord as easily as she could discuss the weather.

When I asked her how she could talk about those incidents without feeling any emotion she simply shrugged. She regarded her ability to be unaffected by the past as healing. She had "gotten over" all the pain of her past. But when I asked her how this healing had occurred, she could not answer.

When Roberta returned for the second session, she said the "healing" had occurred one day around age ten when her father beat her for crying. At that moment she just refused to hurt anymore and that was that. Now, the past was gone and she saw no need to discuss it. If it didn't bother her and she seldom thought about it, why bring it up?

Roberta had repressed her past and with it all of her ability to feel.

In our third session, Roberta finally made an emotional connection with her past. Painful memories came rushing back, and she began to shake. She dropped therapy shortly after that, preferring her cold world to the pain of being alive.

I feel much misinformation and fear has been generated lately about the subject of repressed memories. Every few weeks another talk show host or other high profile personality is publishing a new book exposing horrible abuse that suddenly popped into their memory. This has made more than a few people suspicious of their own mind. I often have clients who fear they were abused but have forgotten about it, and when I am fielding questions from a group I am frequently asked if the fact that a person can't remember the sixth grade means something secret and terrible happened that year.

Explore your own fear of repressed abuse memories by checking any of the following statements as they apply to your situation.

1. ☐ I have heard of repressed memories, but I don't believe such a thing is really possible.

2. ☐ I am somewhat concerned about the possibility of abuse memories coming to light as I work through this book, but I am willing to continue.

3. ☐ I have unclear memories of abuse, and I am frightened at what I might find.

4. ☐ I am afraid that I was sexually abused and that forgotten memories are hidden in my brain.

5. ☐ I am not at all concerned about repressed memories and feel that I have clear memories of all the important events of my life.

Although repression is a true phenomenon, sudden, shocking awareness of previously unknown abuse memories is very rare. I won't go so far as to say that no one ever went through their life believing that they came from a loving family and then on their thirtieth birthday remembered that their father raped them, but I will say that documentation of such cases seems very rare.

It is far more common for someone to be disconnected from the pain of abuse memories (like Roberta). Also, repression can be seen in people who have only foggy, distant memories. A mist has obscured the past, but they still know they were abused. When they get into therapy, frozen emotions begin to thaw and memories become clearer, but this is an expansion of awareness rather than being new information that shocks the client.

THREE BATTLEFIELDS OF REJECTION

Julia, Sheila, and Roberta are real people. Each story was taken from my case files and although names and details have been changed, their stories are true. I could have chosen any number of other cases, but I chose these three for special reasons. Each story was clear and interesting, and each was fought on a different battlefield as well as with a different war tactic.

Julia used the tactic of stuck-in-the-muck in a war on the battlefield of genetic heritage. Sheila used suppression on the battlefield of choice. And Roberta used the war tactic of repression to fight on the battlefield of her environment.

The following chart may help us to see the three battlefields of rejection and the three war tactics of rejection more clearly.

THREE BATTLEFIELDS OF SELF-REJECTION

	Genetic	Choice	Environment
Stuck-in-the-muck	Julia's big feet		
Suppression		Sheila's decision to leave school	
Repression			Roberta's abuse

Genetics

Let's look at Julia's battlefield: Genetics. Julia's feet were part of her birthright. They came to her unasked for, unplanned, and unchangeable. They were a part of her genetic heritage like her eye color. While it is obviously futile to fight against genetics, Julia is not alone in choosing that battlefield. Most of us fight at least a skirmish or two on that field at some time in our life.

Our genetic heritage came to us when we were conceived. We didn't ask for it. We can't change it. Genetics decided our race, the texture of our hair, our basic intelligence, athletic ability, whether we are male or female, and much more.

Most of us have trouble accepting our genetics during the years of adolescence when our bodies are changing without our permission, but for some of us difficulty with genetic acceptance is a lifelong fight. The genetic battlefield can involve such diverse issues as eating disorders, embarrassment over the menstrual process, inability to accept our aging, and sexual dysfunction.

Choice

Our identity is unavoidably wrapped up in our choices—good choices and bad. We express ourselves through our choices: from the clothes we wear to the decision to marry or have a child. Examining choice is one way of discovering who we are.

The area of choice is one of the most common and most difficult areas of self-rejection because dealing with it successfully requires that we face our responsibility of choice squarely and forgive ourselves when we blow it.

Sheila fought against her choices and refused to take responsibility for the decisions she had made.

Environment

The third battlefield of rejection is our environment. This area includes all those uncontrollable things that happen to us without our choice. The home we grew up in, job opportunities or lack of them, a church split, and physical illness; these are part of our environment.

The fact that our environment can be both painful and beyond our control forces us to face some difficult theological realities. Questions such as, How can a good God and a bad world coexist? and, If God is all-powerful and loves us, how come these painful times are allowed? will have to be honestly faced before we can accept an environment that so often seems cruel and without logic.

A FINAL WORD

The central premise of this guide is that we lost ourselves through self-rejection and we can only find ourselves again by identifying those elements of self that we cast aside and learning to accept them as part of our unchangeable reality allowed by God. That premise only takes one sentence to say, but it can take years to implement.

I can take the stories of Julia, Sheila, and Roberta and strip them of complex details, condense twenty sessions of therapy into one paragraph, and plot it on a chart to simplify and communicate a basic principle. But real people and real life don't often fit comfortably on charts. Life is not that simple.

The next three sections will be encouraging you to look at your own genetic heritage, environmental realities, and choices. These three sections are the heart of this guidebook. Their purpose is self-discovery.

Yet self-discovery is not the end. We must move on past that to an acceptance of self. Like Hansel picking up stones, we find these things in order to lead us back home. We want to find a place where the walls are gone and the fog has cleared, a place where we can relax and be ourselves because we know and accept ourselves.

Finish this chapter by writing a personal summation. Some questions you may want to consider: How could I describe in my own words the author's idea of the judgment-shame-rejection-isolation cycle? Which exercise had the deepest emotional impact on me? Can I identify specific areas where I might have rejected pieces of myself? As I work through this book, am I seeing myself or someone else in the examples? Am I afraid of the exposure if I stop hiding? Which method of hiding do I most often use, stuck-in-the-muck, suppression, or repression?

Personal Summation:

PART TWO

Genetics, the Biological Self

CHAPTER 4 ❧

My Link in the Family Chain

As we journey backward, picking up the discarded pieces of our lives, one of the first things we notice is that we are not alone. Our lives are inextricably entwined with many other lives.

As we begin to learn why we decided to cast off pieces of ourselves, we see that truly "No man is an island unto himself alone." In recording our emotional responses to the actions of others, remembering the good and the bad, we start to see the pattern of interactions with others. We will begin by focusing on our biological connections.

Each of us is endowed with our own unique set of genetic information, passed down to us through a long line stretching back for centuries. It is a vital part of our identity. We didn't ask for it. We can't change it. But it is a major factor in our self-image. When we are ashamed of something we were given at birth, like our height or intelligence or skin color, we will have trouble accepting ourselves.

Only last night I was in a late appointment with a client struggling with depression and low self-esteem. This was our fourth meeting, and I felt we had built enough trust for me to approach what I suspected was a very tender issue. "Tell me how you feel about your race," I asked. He immediately dropped his eyes and hardened. "I hate being Japanese. I would rather be white." I was saddened by his answer because I knew the uphill battle he would face trying to accept himself when he rejected the skin color he saw in the mirror.

Our genetics determine many things including our bodily characteristics, basic temperament, level of intelligence, and some scientists even suspect the date and manner of our death may come to us through our genetics.

In this chapter we will look at our genetic link—the family. We will examine how emotional problems and patterns of dysfunction may have been passed down to us from previous generations.

IF YOU ARE ADOPTED

If you are adopted, you are in good company. Moses, the prophet Samuel, and our Lord Jesus Christ were also adopted. Being raised by someone other than your biological parents is not something new.

However, adoption presents special challenges as you work through this chapter because you have two families that have impacted your life. Your biological family gave you your genetic heritage, and your adopted family gave you a large part of your environmental heritage.

Your environmental heritage will be discussed in a later section; for now, we will focus on your genetic heritage. If you have little or no knowledge of your biological family, you may think the exercises concerning genetic heritage do not apply to you, but they do.

Just like every child ever born, you have a genetic heritage and a biological family. Adoption does not change that. You are connected by birth and blood to other people. You may know a lot about your biological family, or you may know nothing at all, but your genetic link to others still exists. Birth would be impossible without it.

The adopted child who may know nothing at all about her birth parents and the blue-blood descendant of royalty have this in common: Both know only part of the whole picture. No one knows all their biological connections, only God knows. A certain mystery remains for all of us.

How comfortable we are with what we do know depends a lot on culture and expectations. One individual may be able to develop a full self-identity without all the blanks being filled, but another may find it necessary to search for more genetic information in order to feel that her identity is complete. We must give ourselves the freedom to search or not according to our private needs.

Your purpose for working these exercises is just the same as those who have generations of family history: We are trying to identify specific areas of rejection. Remember, it is very possible to reject the family you never met.

If you are adopted, you might consider working the exercises twice—once with your biological family and once with your adopted family.

Begin this chapter by remembering the family connections that others told you existed. How similar are you to others who share part of your same genetic heritage? Complete the following sentences.

1. I was told that I looked like _____.

2. When others got upset with me, they told me I was acting just like _____.

3. The first time I remember seeing my own face was when _____.

4. The person in the family who I feel I resemble most is _____.

5. When I was told that I looked like _____ I felt _____.

6. When I was told that I was acting like _____
   I felt _____.

7. At times I catch myself saying the same words and using the
   same tone of voice as _____.

8. When I look at picture albums of the family I feel _____
   _____.

SOUR APPLES ON THE FAMILY TREE

Investigating our genetic heritage would not be a problem if all our relatives were stable, loving people with whom we had joyful connections, but for most of us this is far from true. There are a few nuts and sour apples on most any family tree, and for some the tree itself can be a continuing source of shame.

I remember when I felt I would never be able to live peacefully unless I could draw my father's blood out of my veins. I did not want that connection. I don't think I was alone in my struggle against the past. In my counseling practice I often encounter people who express a desire to disown a brother or child or pretend that their mother is dead when she is actually living across town.

The problem is that when we reject our family, we are rejecting part of our reality and heritage. God does not expect us to always approve of the way others act. We don't have to feel warm and cozy when a difficult relative crosses our path. We don't have to loan them money or have our picture taken for the morning paper with our arm around their shoulder. But we are obligated to love them, pray for them, and accept their existence in our life as part of God's plan for us. Personally, I don't think I ever really found myself until I accepted my father.

The following exercise may help you identify symptoms of genetic rejection in your life. Check those that apply to you, and as you work, remember: You can reject someone you have never met as easily as you can reject someone close to you. You can reject the father who abandoned you and hate the mother you never saw.

Check those statements that apply to you.

1. ☐ I have never felt like a part of my family.

2. ☐ I avoid talking about one member of my family. When their name comes up, I just walk away.

3. ☐ I find myself revealing family secrets to casual acquaintances even when I don't mean to.

4. ☐ I feel I have a right to reject my family because they rejected me first.

5. ☐ I frequently think over hurts of the past and relive what one of my relatives did to me.

6. ☐ Words like *mom* or *dad* or *sister* stick in my throat when I use them to refer to people in my family.

7. ☐ Holidays are painful, and I can't wait for certain family members to leave.

8. ☐ Sometimes I feel homesick, but going back to be around family doesn't help.

9. ☐ I am embarrassed to let people know about my family.

10. ☐ I sometimes pretend to have a different racial background.

11. ☐ I really don't care to think about my family and find this chapter very uncomfortable.

12. ☐ I keep waiting for my family to accept me, but they never have.

13. ☐ I have tried for years to fix my family and draw them together, but they always resist me.

14. ☐ Everything I have ever tried to do for my family was wasted effort.

THE PRETEND FAMILY

Rejection is war. Sometimes in our attempt to reject reality, we try to create a facade to hide the truth from ourselves and others. Larry Crabb expressed this when he said, "The results of the Fall include separation not only from God and from others, but also from ourselves. We come apart as persons, unable to genuinely accept ourselves as we are. Our consequent struggle to be or to pretend to be what we are not explains much of our deep discontent and personal suffering."

This pretending is sometimes in the church family.

The Bible often talks about the family of God. Terms like *brother*, *sister*, or *spiritual father* are part of our rich heritage in the Lord. We can use words like *sister Beth* and *brother Joe* because they describe a reality of spirit that God has given to us. They can express our responsibility toward and our feelings for each other. In this context they are good and true and bonding. But they can also be used in a less-than-holy attempt to set up a pseudofamily to replace a real family that we reject.

I have been surprised at the number of Christians who try to set up a pretend family. They will find a friend and try to make them a pretend "sister" or "big brother," or they will "adopt" a neighborhood child. They will often find an older Christian to call "mom" or "dad." Yet the sour fruit that is produced by these relationships lets us know that they are not healthy affirmations of the family of God; instead, they are lame efforts of the flesh to invent a "new" family to replace the real family which they inwardly reject.

This sour fruit will often show itself in one of two ways: Either these relationships will be stormy and short-lived, or one individual will drain the other in an attempt to gain self-worth and self-identity from the relationship.

These relationships may be brief, such as when a new member breezes into a group and quickly becomes attached to one or two individuals. There is great rejoicing as the new member marvels at the love she has found and exclaims that no one in her life has ever been as wonderful as this new family. But within a few months (or sometimes only weeks) the new member is feeling betrayed and disappointed that her new family is not meeting her needs. She openly criticizes their treatment of her. An explosion follows, and she is off to find another support group, church, or Bible study group she can make into another pretend family for a while.

The other sour fruit hangs on the tree much longer. We see this fruit when a person finds a "sister," "mother," or "big brother" to lean on and just keeps leaning. They are good at putting guilt on others for not being what a Christian "should" be. And for them, the "should" means, "Others should meet all my needs and I should be the baby that always takes and never gives."

In a very real sense, the church is a family and we are a brotherhood of Christians. Because we are joined by the Spirit of God, we have a deep connection that marks us and sets us apart from the rest of creation. "God sets the solitary in families" (Ps. 68:6).

But like good earthly families, the church family is not all sweetness and candy. There is a toughness and a tenacity that clings to reality and forces growth. The church is not a pretend family, but a real one because of the joint Spirit that connects each individual to all others.

THE
GENOGRAM

When we ask, Who am I and where did I come from?, we presuppose a genetic link to the past. Counselors have designed a way to get a quick and complete look at that genetic link through the use of a genogram.

A genogram can help you get a sense of the flow of life and discover patterns of behavior in your family. It is similar to a family tree but is designed to be more than that. It shows each individual's place in the family and lets us examine how different members have affected the system. It also helps us to see the role assumed by the family members in their interaction with one another.

The following exercise is somewhat different from the others in the guidebook because it is longer and more involved. You will work on scrap paper first, then transfer your findings to a special page provided at the end of the chapter.

I would encourage you to use a pencil so you will be able to erase if you need to make changes.

You will be led through the construction of your personal genogram as we watch the development of a fictitious genogram for Carol Frankland, but don't let your work be dictated by only the examples given. Make your personal genogram as large or as small as you want. I have seen clients bring genograms into the office on large sheets of butcher paper that spread all the way across the office floor, but have also worked on a limited genogram with a client during part of a session and was able to fit the entire genogram onto one sheet of typing paper.

You will find the completed genogram for Carol on page 66 and a set of genogram symbols on page 71. Refer to these if you have questions.

We start the genogram by recording Carol's full name and the date that we are taking this "picture" of her life. We will identify males with square symbols and females with circles. Because

Genogram Example: #1

Carol Denise Frankland   Fall—1993

Carol is the focus of our study, we will put a double circle around her. We would have used a double box for a male. Carol's current age is recorded inside the circle along with her name.

Following the example above, begin working on your own genogram using scrap paper.

Genogram Example: #2

Carol Denise Frankland   Fall—1993

Carol was married to Bob in 1969. If you are married or have been married, connect your symbol with that of your husband or ex-husband noting his name and current age. If you have been married more than once, include only your first husband at this point.

Carol was the second of three children. She has an older sister, Chris, and a younger brother, Carl. Her mother's name is Valery, and her father's name is Joe. Joe died in 1968 at age forty-five.

Continue working on your own genogram as you add parents and brothers or sisters if you have them. Later we will add stepparents, step-siblings, half-brothers, and half-sisters. For now, include only your completely biological connections.

Genogram Example: #3

Carol Denise Frankland   Fall—1993

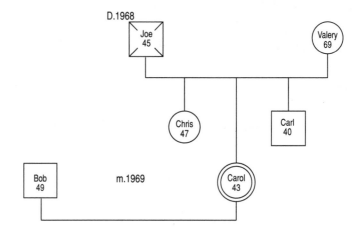

Genogram Example: #4

Carol Denise Frankland   Fall—1993

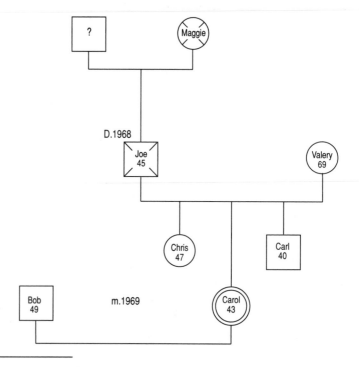

Tracing back another generation on Carol's genogram, we have recorded very little about her grandparents; we know that her paternal grandmother, Maggie, has died, and we know nothing about her paternal grandfather.

We can continue to go farther back, adding great-grandparents using the same system already developed, or we can add notes and dates of important events or memories. As a general rule, genograms should cover at least three generations.

Carol and Bob have two children. A boy, Ronnie, who is now twenty-one and a girl, Joyce, who is nineteen. Carol was preg-

Genogram Example: #5

Carol Denise Frankland   **Fall—1993**

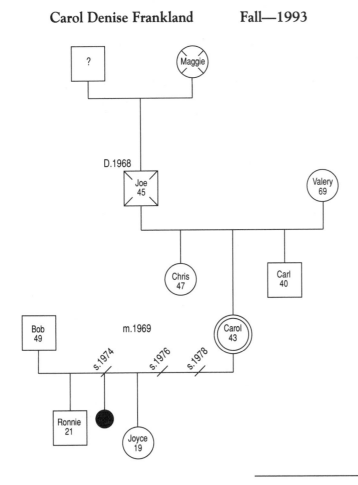

nant with a third child between Ronnie and Joyce. She and her husband were separated at the time and Carol aborted the baby. Had Carol's baby been stillborn or miscarried naturally, the same solid circle would have been used to indicate the baby's life and place in the family. The single strokes through the marriage line show times and dates of separation.

By providing more space between Carol's siblings, we could have recorded their spouses and Carol's nieces and nephews. If these relationships had been significant, or if we had simply been curious and wanted to get a complete picture, we would have included that information. As you work, record as much as you want and as much as you believe necessary to give yourself an overall picture of your family heritage.

Carol's mother married a second time in 1980. Her husband's name is Jim. In this same year, Carol and Bob divorced. One year later, Carol married a second time.

Add divorces and multiple marriages to your personal genogram following the example on page 65. Include half-brothers and half-sisters with the proper parental heritage.

Dates often provide significant information as to how certain events may have affected your life. We did not write it on the genogram, but a little math will show that Carol was born in 1950. She would have been eighteen at the time of her father's death and we note that she married Bob at nineteen. We could ask if the loss of her father had any impact on Carol's decision to marry. When she chose Bob, a man six years her senior, was she somehow looking for a replacement for her father? Did those dynamics have any bearing on the fact that Carol and Bob were separated three times before divorcing after eleven years?

As you construct your own genogram, try to look at your life as a whole. What questions and coincidences do you notice? Work slowly, taking time to remember and date significant events.

Continuing on the genogram, we see that Carol and Mark have adopted a daughter, Connie. She is eight. For the past several years, Carol's teenage daughter by her first marriage has been giving them a lot of trouble. She quit school at seventeen

Genogram Example: #6

Carol Denise Frankland **Fall—1993**

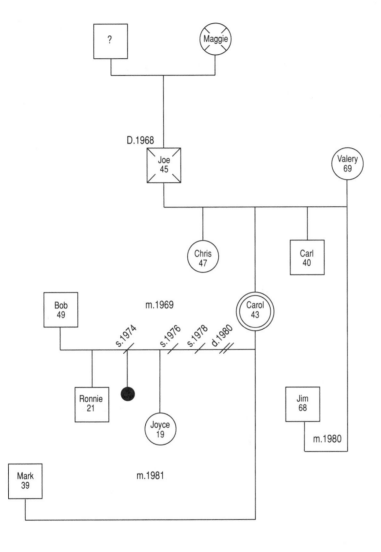

and moved in with her boyfriend, Wayne. Wayne and Joyce have a one-month-old daughter, Jennifer, and despite Carol's efforts to stop the relationship, she is now a grandmother. We have also added some of Mark's history to the genogram.

You will notice that this genogram contains some new symbols in the form of the letters *P.A.* and *A.A.* A genogram not only records biological relations, but any significant information that impacts the family. Symbols for physical abuse (P.A.), alcohol

Genogram Example: #7

Carol Denise Frankland   Fall—1993

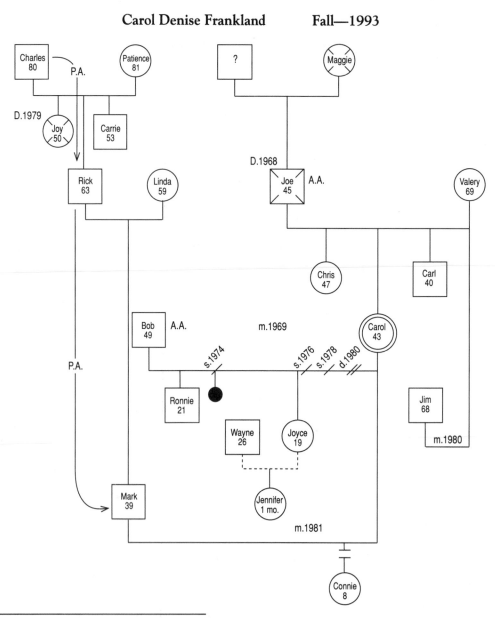

abuse (A.A.), sexual abuse (S.A.), verbal abuse (V.A.), and drug abuse (D.A.) can be placed on the chart beside the name of the person affected or between two people with arrows showing the direction of the abuse.

In Carol's genogram, we can see that her father was involved in alcohol abuse and so was her first husband, Bob. There is physical abuse running through Mark's family as Charles abused his son, Rick, and Rick in turn abused Mark.

The reason we mark these things is to trace the transmittance of family problems from one generation to the next. This gives us the opportunity to break the pattern so that it is not passed to the next generation. We can also predict who may be at risk.

If I were a therapist working with this family I would want to very carefully investigate the possible risks to Connie. She could inherit abuse from her father, Mark; her mother, Carol, has a history of being involved with dysfunctional men. Unless something happens to stop the cycles of abuse and dysfunction—such as Mark developing a strong relationship with the Lord or Carol recognizing her dysfunctional patterns and seeking treatment—the risk to Connie is significant.

I would also wonder about Joyce and Wayne. Is she repeating a pattern of being addicted to men similar to that of her mother and grandmother?

After you have finished your basic genogram, transfer it to page 68. You can continue your work on separate paper adding as much as you want, but this book will probably not hold everything you desire to put down.

There is no limit to what information can be included on a genogram. Significant events such as a house fire, bankruptcy, or major surgery can be added and dated. Illness can be traced. Relationships can be drawn between people using either the symbols on page 71 or your own. You can use various colors on your genogram if you like. Notes can be added beside names to indicate significant information about personalities and relationships.

Your genogram should give you a clear picture of your history and life connections, and it should help you see what part of your God-given heritage you may be rejecting. Use it to help you complete the sentences at the end of this chapter. It can also be used to spark your thinking as you work the next section of the workbook which focuses on how you have been shaped by your environment.

Your Personal Genogram Record

I have used Carol Frankland's genogram to complete the five statements below. Use your own genogram to help you complete the fifteen statements on the personal summation page at the end of this chapter. Use extra paper if you want to add more statements.

Carol Frankland

1. I am a woman who has been married twice.

2. I am the second daughter of Valery Brooks.

3. I am a grandmother.

4. I am a child of an alcoholic father.

5. I am the mother of two live children and one aborted child.

 *Personal Summation:*

1. I am _____
   _____.

2. I am _____
   _____.

3. I am _____
   _____.

4. I am _____
   _____.

5. I am _____
   _____.

6. I am _____
   _____.

7. I am _____
   _____.

8. I am _____
   _____.

9. I am _____
   _____.

10. I am _____
    _____.

11. I am _____
    _____.

12. I am _____
    _____.

13. I am _____
    _____.

14. I am _____
    _____.

15. I am _____
    _____.

Genogram Symbols

 Female

 Male

 Marriage

 Deceased female

 Adopted female

 Twin males

Stillbirth or abortion

Divorce

Separation

B. (date)   Date of birth

D. (date)   Date of death

m. (date)   Date of marriage

s. (date)   Date of separation

d. (date)   Date of divorce

Abbreviations of Abuse

P.A.   Physical Abuse

A.A.   Alcohol Abuse

V.A.   Verbal Abuse

D.A.   Drug Abuse

S.A.   Sexual Abuse

Relationship Symbols

 Antagonistic / hostile relationship

Live in / loose relationship

Broken / emotionally divorced relationship

Close relationship

Codependent / too close relationship

❧ CHAPTER 5

My Body and My Personality

Our journey into the past includes a look at our own body. It is the body that first makes us aware of our existence. Often, our first experience of shame involves our body; we begin to reject what we cannot change.

If you have watched a baby discover her own hand, you have seen the wonder in the little one's eyes as she realizes that the fist moving back and forth is under her control. What a powerful feeling that must be for a newborn! Later, she will find a foot is also attached to the package God gave her; "open mouth, insert foot" becomes a delightful reality for an infant before it becomes a warning to loose-tongued adults!

There was a day when we, too, first discovered we had feet attached to our legs. Later we learned to control bowel and bladder action; and for most of us that was a big step, proving our control of ourselves and our world.

Still later, we discovered our limitations as we met other children who could run faster or hit harder. Then somewhere between the ages of ten and fifteen, our bodies developed sexual characteristics, and many of us had strong feelings about what our bodies were doing to us. If we were athletic, we may have learned we could push, shape, or train what God had given us and get praise from people for what our bodies could do or how they looked.

And as the years pass, we continue to discover what our bodies will and won't do as they keep changing, sometimes in ways we may think undesirable; weight, wrinkles, graying hair, aging, and death are also part of body change and discovery.

Our body is a completely individualized earth suit in which our soul has been wrapped. It was given to us by God. It is temporary and will wear out in about seventy-five to eighty-five years. Although it is a miracle of machinery and creation, it is also flawed by sin and damaged by choice and time. These realities make the body somewhat less than we might desire.

This marvelous and limited, wonderful and painful box in which we live was given to us through the bloodline we saw on our genogram. We received it at conception, and its individual features are controlled by a central system as features for a computer are determined by the software. Our genetic "software" is called the DNA molecule.

One of the advantages of entering college as an adult is that you have experienced enough of the difficulties of life to appreciate the wonders, and one of the things that I found most wonder-filled was a chart at the front of the biology lab. Younger students passed it by with scarcely a glance, or they studied it in a pragmatic fashion to prepare for a test. But being a grandma in her forties attending her first college lab class, I found it fascinating.

The chart looked like a long ladder twisted into a spiral. On each rung of the ladder, a pink ball on the left was connected to a blue ball on the right. The balls marched up the outside edges of the ladder two by two, each one with his mate. This was a scientist's model of the DNA.

At the moment of conception, the long string of pink balls (representing the genetic contribution of the mother) is matched with the long string of blue balls (representing the genetic contribution of the father), and a new life is set in motion.

For the sake of any physicians or biologists among my readers, I concede that calling the DNA our genetic software may be an oversimplification, but not by much. This tiny molecule is the program that controls and shapes our biological life. We can't change it, we didn't choose it, and only death will stop it. In fact, some theorize that the timing of death itself may be programmed on the DNA.

Scientists are constantly making new discoveries about DNA, but most of the information remains unknown. We do know that everything about our body, our natural talent, and our brain is programmed on the DNA.

Now you will discover some of the things you are because of the genetic coding that God gave you. Some of these things may have been altered by choice (example: you may have changed the color of your hair), or they may have been altered by circumstance (example: your impulsive nature may have been sobered by discipline), but the basic system you were born with remains.

We will discuss choice and environment later; for now, fill in the blanks with a short phrase about your opinions concerning your genetic coding. Choose your own words and don't necessarily limit yourself to the obvious or to those suggestions provided in parentheses.

1. My race/nationality is (Caucasian, Irish, African-American, Hispanic, Asian, American Indian) _____.

2. I would describe my fingernails as being (ugly, strong, beautifully shaped, easily cracked) _____.

3. I developed sexually (sooner, later, about the same time) _____ as most of the other kids I knew.

4. I have always found math or anything to do with numbers to be (easy, impossible) _____.

5. When it comes to music I am (naturally talented, can't carry a tune) _____.

6. I am a (male, female) _____.

7. My sense of humor is (dry, quick and easy, nonexistent) _____.

8. I am most comfortable around (things, people) _____ _____.

9. My feet fit in a size _____ shoe.

10. My eyes (are getting weak, are blue, have been crossed since I was a kid) _____.

11. When I gain weight, it has a tendency to gather around my _____.

12. The color of my hair is _____.

13. It appears to me that I am aging (about the same, with more pain, more slowly) _____ than most people I know.

14. My natural intelligence is probably (above average, average, below average) _____.

By looking at your answers, you can get some idea of how important your genetic coding has been in shaping you into the person you are today. To a large extent, as far as this physical world goes, you *are* your DNA. How deeply and peacefully you accept all these attributes, which you did not request, will determine how well you accept yourself.

You may have noticed the list above included more than physical characteristics. It also included characteristics of temperament and intelligence. These attributes were also given to us at birth.

As we use this chapter to discover what we have been given and how we have embraced or rejected those gifts, I have chosen to divide our inquiry into two parts; one concerns the physical and the other concerns the unseen part of our biological heritage, the temperament.

O U R   B O D Y

Our bodies have been constantly evaluated by ourselves and others since we were born. From the day we were born, when the nurse held us squirming and yawning up to the nursery window, and someone said, "He has eyes just like uncle Joe!" we have been identified with the bodies we live in and how well they work.

Embarrassment over being physically inadequate or different begins very early. Little children take great pride in being the tallest or biggest or fastest, and the most common compliment a little girl gets is about her body: "My, isn't she pretty?" Children quickly notice what is valued, and they just as quickly learn to compare themselves with others, struggling with shame if they believe that comparison shows them lacking.

Rejection of the Body

Rejection of the body God gave us is very common. For some of us the rejection is mild and passing, but for many of us the distress can be severe or even life-threatening, as in the case of eating disorders.

To test how well you have accepted your body, stand before a mirror totally naked. Really look for a moment at the body God gave you. Can you thank Him for everything you see? Are you comfortable with the image that looks back at you from the glass? For some people, even the idea of standing naked before a mirror is very distressing; this is a strong indication of body rejection.

Remember the three forms of rejection. If something about your body (your weight, a scar, your age, etc.) is distressing, or a memory of negative comments others have made frequently occupies your mind, or if you find yourself making jokes about your body, or calling attention to something that embarrasses you, you may be rejecting the body God gave you by being stuck-in-the-muck.

If you are self-conscious about your body and fearful of what others are thinking or saying about it, or if you try to hide your body from others, or if you fight against these fears and pretend they are not there, you may be rejecting the body God gave you by suppressing.

If you now have no emotional connection to an event that was once shameful to you because you were physically violated or abused, if there is a deadness of soul or other symptoms which would suggest that the problem is still there, you may be rejecting the body God gave you by repressing.

Our bodies are part of our identity. Our sexuality, our looks, our capabilities, our limitations, our illnesses are expressed with or contained in the body. Acceptance of the body is acceptance of reality. This acceptance should be done with respect because this body is the only box God has loaned us to carry our souls around in from here to the resurrection.

Our perception of our body is not always accurate. Often children perceive themselves as fat, different, ugly, or short when in reality they are none of these things. How did you perceive your body as a child?

_____

Write a physical description of how you perceived yourself as a child or young teen.

_____
_____
_____
_____

Do you view yourself differently now, as you look back through family pictures?

_____

If so, how?

_____

_____

Those Terrible Teens

Around the time of puberty our bodies begin to change with no warning. If we haven't found something to reject about our bodies before this time, we certainly will by the time adolescence is underway.

These intermediate or junior high years are a time of amazing change. Parents are knocked off balance as they try to deal with a child one day and then with an adult the next. The adolescents themselves are challenged to the limit as they wake up in a slightly different body every day.

Girls start the maturity cycle about two years earlier than boys, as they begin to mature sexually while the boys are still concentrating on growing taller.

In this time of change and confusion almost no one is "normal," and many are far enough off the "normal" range to feel very uncomfortable. Counselors recognize that some patterns of difficulty can be predicted as we look at those who mature earlier than their classmates and those who mature later.

If we were listing those expected to experience more difficulty and those who will likely have less, it would be as follows:

1. Early maturing boy   Least difficulty
2. Late maturing girl   Moderate difficulty
3. Early maturing girl   Strong difficulty
4. Late maturing boy   Most difficulty

Do you consider yourself to have been in one of these categories? Which one?

Write in detail about your feelings as you watched your body change from day to day, making you different from your classmates. Or if you watched the bodies of those around you change while yours remained childlike, describe how you felt about that. Use additional paper if needed.

_____

_____

_____

_____

_____

_____

_____

_____

_____

_____

The shame or satisfaction we feel concerning our bodies is not only determined by our own opinions but also by what others tell us about our bodies and by how our bodies are treated by others. Below is a list of significant people and a list of words to describe the messages these people may have given you about your body. Circle all words that apply.

My father gave me the message that my body was:

inadequate	beautiful	the wrong sex	respected
too weak	sexy	shameful	safe
a gift from God	to be admired	to be used	to be hidden
a problem	an embarrassment	dirty	strong and athletic
my own private property			

My mother gave me the message that my body was:

inadequate	beautiful	the wrong sex	respected
too weak	sexy	shameful	safe
a gift from God	to be admired	to be used	to be hidden
a problem	an embarrassment	dirty	strong and athletic
my own private property			

My church gave me the message that my body was:

inadequate	beautiful	the wrong sex	respected
too weak	sexy	shameful	safe
a gift from God	to be admired	to be used	to be hidden
a problem	an embarrassment	dirty	strong and athletic
my own private property			

My first boyfriend gave me the message that my body was:

inadequate   beautiful   the wrong sex   respected
too weak   sexy   shameful   safe
a gift from God   to be admired   to be used   to be hidden
a problem   an embarrassment   dirty   strong and athletic
my own private property

My _____ gave me the message that my body was:

inadequate   beautiful   the wrong sex   respected
too weak   sexy   shameful   safe
a gift from God   to be admired   to be used   to be hidden
a problem   an embarrassment   dirty   strong and athletic
my own private property

My _____ gave me the message that my body was:

inadequate   beautiful   the wrong sex   respected
too weak   sexy   shameful   safe
a gift from God   to be admired   to be used   to be hidden
a problem   an embarrassment   dirty   strong and athletic
my own private property

My _____ gave me the message that my body was:

inadequate   beautiful   the wrong sex   respected
too weak   sexy   shameful   safe
a gift from God   to be admired   to be used   to be hidden
a problem   an embarrassment   dirty   strong and athletic
my own private property

Review the exercises you have completed to this point. What were you feeling as you answered each question? Are there things about your physical life that make you ashamed? Have you rejected the self God gave you by rejecting and fighting against a physical reality that you could not change? If so, use the space below to write a prayer to God. Tell Him that you now want to accept all He made you to be in the physical world.

Prayer:

OUR PERSONALITY AND TEMPERAMENT

Not only are the physical parts of our body guided by our DNA, but other, more abstract things seem to be affected as well—our personality, our mental capability, and the way we relate to the world. It is a matter of heated debate as to exactly where the line can be drawn between biology and training, but few professionals would deny that biological endowment plays a significant role.

Parents who have several children would probably agree with the scientists as they watch their children, who were raised in the same way, turn out so very different from one another. One child lands in the delivery room griping about every procedure while another child is compliant and easy to handle from the first breath. One child will melt when talked to in a displeased tone of voice while the other will defy authority to the bitter end.

As you consider your own life and how your biological heritage has shaped who you are, consider your temperament as well as your physical characteristics.

In order to help you identify this part of your genetic heritage, complete the following.

Below is a list of self-descriptive adjectives. Circle those that best describe who you are by temperament and how you relate to others in your world now.

active	ambitious	self-confident	persistent
nervous	hardworking	impatient	impulsive
moody	melancholy	excitable	imaginative
calm	serious	easygoing	shy
good-natured	introverted	extroverted	likable
leader	quiet	hard-boiled	fearful
submissive	self-conscious	lonely	sensitive
dependent	observant	fun-loving	

Are there other significant words that describe you now?

_____

_____

Now think of yourself as a child. Using a second list of the same words, circle those that describe your personality at that time.

active	ambitious	self-confident	persistent
nervous	hardworking	impatient	impulsive
moody	melancholy	excitable	imaginative
calm	serious	easygoing	shy
good-natured	introverted	extroverted	likable
leader	quiet	hard-boiled	fearful
submissive	self-conscious	lonely	sensitive
dependent	observant	fun-loving	

Are there other significant words that could be used to describe you as a child?

_____

_____

Compare the two lists. Are there some words that could have described you as a child, but also describe you as an adult? List them below.

_____

_____

_____

_____

Because biological endowment remains stable over time, the temperament you were given at conception would probably show little change through the years. Words that appear on both lists probably indicate your core temperament. If the lists were extremely different and no words were used twice, your natural temperament may have been overpowered by a harsh or restrictive environment in childhood or by the environment in which you now live.

Now turn your attention to the way you relate to others and life in general. Again, we look first at the adult and then at the child. Complete the sentences in your own words.

When there are a lot of other people around, I

_____

_____

_____

When I am angry, I

_____

_____

_____

When being introduced to others, I feel

_____

_____

_____

When someone hurts me, I respond by

_____

_____

_____

When I am afraid, I

_____

_____

_____

One thing I really enjoy is

_____

_____

_____

Now complete the following sentences which are similar to the first set. Answer them according to your experiences as a child, connecting the sentences with specific memories if you can.

When there were many people around, I would

_____

_____

_____

When I got angry, I expressed it by

_____

_____

_____

When meeting new people (such as going to a new school, etc.), I often felt

_____

_____

_____

When someone hurt my feelings, I would

_____

_____

_____

When I was afraid, I

_____

_____

_____

My favorite way to play as a child was

_____

_____

_____

This would normally be the point where we would compare the two lists and I would ask you to try and describe the natural temperament that God gave you at birth; however, we have a problem with temperament that we do not face with the physical endowment. We must take time to identify the differences between natural temperament and sin.

Is It Temperament or Is It Sin?

One of the challenges we face in trying to discover our temperament is determining which qualities are God-given and which are sinful. The problem arises because all temperaments can be sinful, but none of them must be sinful. An easygoing, lighthearted temperament can lead to a refusal to take anything seriously and an avoidance of life, but it does not have to. A born leader who likes making decisions and being out front can become a tyrant who listens to no one, but she does not have to.

We should never excuse sin by saying, "That is just the way I am." No, you are not that way. You have allowed your natural bent to lead you astray and failed to let Christ conform the raw material of your birth into His image.

We must always stand against sin and reject its presence in our life, but we dare not reject the natural bent of our temperament or we will be rejecting a gift from God.

It is not always easy to tease out sin from natural temperament, but perhaps the difference between the two and how the Spirit can give us wisdom and discernment to identify that difference can best be illustrated by a client I recently saw in the office.

Kathlene was a natural actress. Artistic, dramatic, emotional, enthusiastic, adventuresome, all could describe this five foot two inch ball of energy. But her father was conservative, authoritarian, old-fashioned, and never traveled far from the place he was born. Needless to say, as Kathlene entered her adult years, father and daughter collided.

All of her life Kathlene had been told that her "flighty" ways and instant emotion were shameful things. It was wrong for her to like big cities and crowds, and she was prideful because she liked to perform. For years she tried to fit her personality into her father's preconceived mold and hated every moment of it, but when she left home and tried her own way, she felt guilty for not being a "good" woman.

Kathlene had to determine what was and was not sin according to the criteria of God's Word, not her emotional reaction or her father's opinion. Nowhere in all the holy Word of God does it say, "Thou shalt not like big cities," nor does it say that enjoying the drama of performance is bad.

However, the Spirit would not let Kathlene stop there. As she continued to pray, she was convicted of the real sins of vengefulness, an unforgiving heart, and a stiff-necked pride that was determined to do everything her way.

But even this step of identifying her sin, confessing it, and forsaking it was only part of the battle. Because of her early training, Kathlene was ashamed of her natural temperament. This made it very difficult for her to live in either the world her father designed for her or the life God designed for her. When she stepped into the mold her earthly father had set, she struggled because it was against her natural bent. When she stepped into the mold her heavenly Father had set, she was haunted by childhood training and her strong desire for approval. The battle to accept and enjoy who she was yet live without sin and rebellion took years to balance out.

We can reject our basic temperament just as easily as we can reject our physical body. The popularity of certain temperaments goes in and out of style as surely as body types and clothing. The artistic, sensitive thinker would be valued by some social circles while the assertive, no-nonsense leader would be valued by others.

Look over the information in the previous two exercises (p. 82). Try to choose three to six words that could describe both the child and the adult. You may use words that have already been listed if they seem to fit best, but you do not have to limit your selection in any way.

Do you feel good about the words you have selected? Would you rather have different, less honest words describe your temperament? Have you let any of your natural tendencies lead you to sin?

THE GIFT OF ME

Our genetics are a priceless gift from a sovereign God. When we reject that natural endowment, we fight against Him and lose our sense of who we are. But that reality quickly brings us up against some of the most complicated theological problems that have plagued mankind since the beginning of time. Can God make a mistake? Do we have any right to change or alter what He has allowed to be?

It is one thing to be asked to accept the fact that we are

shorter than we wanted to be or that we have never been musically talented, but what about accepting the fact that we were born with a heart problem that made us housebound most of our life? What about defective hands or a mind that refuses to work correctly? What about a natural temperament that is painfully shy or a strong desire to lead and shape the world when you are also a woman? Are we supposed to accept these things too?

I believe the unflinching answer to those questions is yes. If it came by birth and we cannot change it, then we must humbly accept God's sovereignty and wait to see how He is going to take that reality and work it out for our good and His glory.

I will not attempt to elaborate on that subject here because it is too broad. You will find some of the answers in Chapter 6 as we look at our genetics from God's perspective, but the final answer must come from you. When you learn to accept life as it is, not as you wish it would be, a peace will slowly begin to dawn, and with that peace will come faith and understanding.

As for our right to alter what our genetic endowment has given us, that will be covered in our section on choice. Here, it will be sufficient to say that if God approves of us using choice to curb the fire of a quick temper and mold it into an energy for defending the truth, I doubt that He is going to frown on our decision to use our freedom of choice to curb the pain of crooked buck teeth and mold them into something we feel more pleasant about.

Complete this chapter by filling in the personal summation page. Some of the things you might consider examining are how much you feel that you have accepted the body and temperament God gave you and how your opinion of who you are may differ from what others have said you should be. Are you willing to accept the limitations God has placed on your body and brain? Are you willing to walk humbly knowing that you did not choose or earn your lot if the natural endowment you were given is admired by others?

Personal Summation:

CHAPTER 6

Did God Really Choose to Make Me?

Our perspective makes all the difference.

Standing up close, we have investigated our genetics by looking at our bodies and our families. We have looked at what we feel and what we think and how we see these realities, but now I want to broaden our view and take a look at our genetic heritage from God's perspective. For this chapter, I hope to "put our eyes" in a different place.

You will need a Bible to work most of the exercises in this chapter. Use any translation with which you are comfortable and can approach with confidence, but the wording in the answers I give will be from the New King James Version unless otherwise indicated.

THE BOTTOM LINE OF HISTORY

In the book of Ephesians Paul, writing under the inspiration of the Holy Spirit, tells us why God bothered with creation in the first place. Like a reporter drawing a deep breath to sum up all the findings in one sentence, or an accountant giving the bottom line to a group of investors, Paul states two reasons for creation—including the creation of you and me.

Look up Ephesians 2:4–7. Here Paul gives two reasons God had for the whole scope of creation and redemption. List those two reasons below.

1. v 4 Because . . . _____

_____

2. v 7 In order that . . . _____

_____

God is using our existence and history to demonstrate His character of love. When we consider our life, our family, our body, our genetic heritage, and we find things we don't like or things we feel are unfair, we can be comforted by knowing that God's love will be demonstrated through us.

One way to think of history is to visualize it as a long bolt of cloth unrolled on the table of eternity, with every individual's life a thread in the fabric. There is the long thread of Methuselah lasting almost one thousand years and the tiny fiber of an unknown baby who died the same day he was born. There is a golden thread of thirty-three years when God Himself became part of the fabric in the form of Jesus Christ. George Washington, an unknown farmer in India, your life, my life, and all other lives are woven together in the same fabric. Each life appears at a certain spot and each disappears at a precise time. This long, multicolored fabric is in a very real sense a proof of who God is and what He is like.

If any being in heaven or hell, now or in eternity, would accuse God of being selfish or cruel, he has only to unroll the fabric of history and silently point to it as proof of His nature of goodness and grace and kindness. We are God's Show-and-Tell.

One point of your identity is that you, too, are part of that great design. Your individual life will be part of the evidence of God's grace.

That huge idea may seem somewhat confusing and contradictory as we stand on our tiny spot in time and stretch our necks trying to see the fabric in its entirety, but this limited view will not be our final perspective.

If you have lived more than thirty years, you have probably already experienced the fantastic difference that time gives to perspective. How strange to look back and see that something we thought vital to life at fifteen matters little to us at twenty-nine. The marriage that we thought would end all our loneliness turns out to be the beginning of loneliness ten years later. The career change that looked like a tragedy turns out to be a financial blessing. How many of us have said, "If I only knew then what I know now. . ."?

If we can experience these shifts in perspective and see clearly in our brief span of years how things look totally different from another angle, is it too big a step of faith to believe that when we are given the eternal perspective and see the cloth as a whole, we will realize the piece of life that so perplexed and irritated us during our stay here was actually a thread of gold woven in for our good and His glory?

That single reality of perspective should make us pause before we cast off an unwelcome piece of ourselves. We might be throwing away one of our greatest treasures.

A PRESENT FOR JESUS

When Paul gives us a look at the end of history and the reasons for our existence, he talks about God's vindication, but earlier in the chapter he speaks of something else—God's feelings and opinion of us. In the first chapter of Ephesians, Paul says that we are presents that God has chosen to pass from His hand to the hand of Jesus, timeless, treasured gifts that are worthy of being given from God to God.

The idea of our being a present to Christ is not symbolic. It is a reality. He says that we are literally presents given to Jesus from God.

If you have consciously given yourself to God, then you are a child of God and He has taken you, along with all other

Christians, and formed you into an inheritance for Christ (Eph. 1:18). All of us together are poured out of the Father's hands and into the hands of Jesus. We are described as "glorious" treasures.

Think of all the other gifts that God could have provided as an inheritance for His Son. Diamond mines, the Rocky Mountains, all the animals in their boundless variety, the planet earth, or all the stars could have been His choice, but He says they are only like chaff for the burning (2 Pet. 3:10). The gift He has chosen is you.

Below you see the hand of God offering a gift to the hand of Jesus. Write your name on the gift box because, in truth, you are inside.

Thoughts about being part of something so vast as the fabric of history or being given as a gift to Jesus may cause you to feel many different emotions. Depending on your background and your trust level at this time, these thoughts may be comforting or frightening, incomprehensible or insulting. Write the feelings you have as you think on these things.

_____

_____

_____

BORN IN THE WRONG TIME AND PLACE

The broad sweep of history can seem rather distant when we, personally, are struggling to accept a family that is an embarrassment or one that has caused us pain. This pain is often reflected in statements like: "I just don't feel like I fit in this family" or "I don't belong here."

I frequently hear clients say they feel like they were born in the wrong time. They are sure their personality and skills would have been much better suited to the Old West or the Middle Ages. They would find it easier to have faith if they could have been born when Jesus was on the earth, or they would not be so nervous if they lived when life was slower, or they long for the adventure of a futuristic life, flying high-tech rockets from planet to planet instead of living with the boredom of corporate America. I am not referring to a romantic notion or a curiosity about another time and place but a deep feeling of discontentment.

And if they are not longing for another time, then my clients at least want a different family. How much better their life would have been if they had been born with a different father! How much easier it would have been if their best friend's mom had been their own!

But can that be true? If another time or a different family would have been better, then your current place in history must be wrong; and if that is true, then God made a mistake.

Don't be too quick to defend God on this point nor fail to look at the question honestly. Don't be afraid to use your head. God's Word does say that the Almighty makes no mistakes (Num. 23:19; James 1:17), and we are obligated to believe that this is true simply by faith in His Word, but God also calls us to reason

(Isa. 1:18) and encourages us to use the brains we have been given as long as we have an honest heart and due respect for the fact that He is God and we are not.

When we consider whether we were born in the wrong time or to the wrong family or whether we would have been more effective, better suited, or better able to serve in a different time and place, we run against a genetic problem that illustrates the absurdity of the question before we even get our elaborate plans for reasoning off the drawing board.

Simply put, it would be impossible for God to allow you to be born anywhere except at the exact time that you were to the exact parents that you have without overriding all natural laws and all history.

The gene pool from which your DNA was selected only existed because your particular mother married your particular father. If you were conceived on any other date you would not exist. The baby born might be your sister or your brother, but not you. You could never have an opportunity to enjoy any other life because your thoughts, feelings, body, and temperament would not exist. Someone else would hold your place.

Of course, God is God and He could override all natural laws and rewrite history for one individual request, but then how could you have made the request before you existed? If God is going to allow earth to roll along according to natural law (and He does), then your birth in the course of natural time and your existence (even though difficult at times) is part of that vast plan and did not take the Almighty by surprise. His own Son was born in the fullness of time (Gal. 4:4) and so were you.

Go back and look at your genogram. Can you thank God for what you see there? That may be very difficult if your genogram contains people who have hurt you.

We are told in the Word that we must be thankful in all things (Eph. 5:20), but all things do not make us happy. It is never that we are thankful for sin or even thankful for pain, but we can be thankful for what pain can produce when we give it to God, and we can be thankful for our existence that provides us with the opportunity to make the future different from the past.

BEATING
THE ODDS

We do not have to depend solely on logic to believe that God had control of our birth. His Word assures us that we are no accident.

When a baby girl is born, her body contains 100,000 to 1 million egg cells (oocytes). Of that number, about 400 cells will develop into mature eggs during a woman's reproductive life (about thirty years). One of those eggs was selected from your mother to become half of your DNA.

Seven to nine male ejaculations contain enough sperm to equal the present population of planet earth. Each of the sperm would make a slightly different individual. If your mother and father had a fairly active sex life during the month you were conceived, one of those 4.5 billion sperms was chosen to become the other half of your DNA.

For you to "win" the right to be born, we must multiply 400/1,000,000 X 1/400 X 1/4,500,000,000. And for that number, we assume your father married your mother and not her sister and that you have your current birthday, not a different one. Considering all the variables we did not figure in, I would guess that if you have been born, you have already beaten greater odds than those of winning the New York Lottery, the Publishers Clearinghouse Sweepstakes, and the Irish Sweepstakes all in the same year.

These mind-boggling statistics do not intimidate God. He assures us that He was well aware of our unique conception.

Due to modern technology and multimillion dollar labs, we have discovered in the last few years that when the genetic material from your mother and the genetic material from your father formed a new individual, the two strings of genetic material were literally woven or knitted together.

It is curious that what we now know about conception was described by David in Psalm 139. Without microscope, without labs, without million-dollar budgets, David talked about a new baby's conception as being woven or knitted together in the womb.

O LORD, you have searched me and you know me. You know when I sit and when I rise: you perceive my thoughts. . . . you are familiar with all my ways. . . .

I praise you because I am fearfully and wonderfully made; . . . My frame was not hidden from you when I was made in the secret place. When I was woven together. . . your eyes saw my unformed body. All the days ordained for me were written in your book before one of them came to be.

How precious to me are your thoughts, O God! How vast is the sum of them! Were I to count them, they would outnumber the grains of sand.

(NIV)

THE BODY

God cares about your body and says specific things about the use and abuse of the body. Check your knowledge on this subject with the following exercise.

Below are several common statements which are attributed to biblical doctrine. Mark each true or false. The correct answers are given at the end of the chapter.

1. Our bodies are an accident of evolution.
   True   False

2. Punishment for sin only takes place in hell, never in the physical body.
   True   False

3. God lives inside our bodies.
   True   False

4. God intentionally made each body different.
   True   False

5. Because Jesus was male, and males were chosen to lead the church and the home, the male body is more valuable than the female body.
   True   False

6. The present body is of this world and can never enter heaven.
   True   False

7. Because the body is not part of our spiritual being, we should not be concerned with its care.
   True   False

8. We will have a body in heaven.
   True   False

9. Our spirit is more important than our body.
   True   False

10. Bodily appetites are sinful.
    True   False

11. Only our spirits can glorify God.
    True   False

12. Neglecting the body is a form of false humility.
    True   False

13. All physical sickness is a punishment from God for sins of the individual.
    True   False

14. Because bodily appetites are so strong, we have no choice but to satisfy them.
    True   False

15. Because bodies are earthly, it is not proper to pray about them unless they are sick.
    True   False

16. There is no one part of the body that, if controlled, will assure control of all other parts of the body.
    True   False

17. The body is a good instrument to be used for serving God.
    True   False

A Living Sacrifice

Not only is our physical life a part of the vast plan of God that will vindicate His character and honor, not only are we a rich and glorious present that God has given to Jesus, not only are we chosen and special because God allowed our particular DNA code to be selected for the privilege of birth, not only was He aware of the intricate processes of our creation and aware of our future before we were born, but there is also another special aspect of the body that is a privilege for humans and humans alone: The chance to take what is naturally unholy and watch it become holy as we offer it as a living sacrifice for His service.

God invites us to present our bodies to Him as living sacrifices (Rom. 12:1). Our hands, feet, mouth, brain, intestines, and spleen can be offered for His control, and He is glad to accept!

As simple and biblical as that concept is, the process of working it out in daily life can be very difficult. Judging from my own experience and the testimony of other Christians, there are three major reasons why we fail in our attempt to become a "living sacrifice."

1. We expect too much from God.
2. We expect too little from ourselves.
3. We expect too much from ourselves.

We expect too much from God.

Sometimes we erroneously assume that if we are a living sacrifice, God moves in like an alien being and takes over our personality, preferences, abilities, and thoughts. Just because we totally yield our body to His service does not mean we cease to exist as individuals. Part of our personhood is our responsibility and our personal desire.

I am reminded of testimony I heard from two very different individuals. One was a woman on a diet in her mid-forties and the other was a young preacher.

The dieter said she wanted to yield her body to God and be healthy and attractive for His glory. Every time she approached a snack or meal she asked God if she should have each bite, then she would look inside trying to find some feeling or inner voice. She frequently felt various inner urges or "voices," but sometimes there was only silence; as a result, she found herself confused and uncertain.

For example, one day she was in the grocery and asked God if she could buy a candy bar: Not eat it, just buy it. Nothing inside felt like "no," so she bought it. In the car she unwrapped it and told God to convict her if eating it were wrong. Nothing. So she ate it and then felt guilty.

It didn't take long before the dieter was very angry with God. She knew she needed to lose weight for health reasons, and she knew how to count calories and fat grams, but she wanted God to do the work. So she kept on eating and complained that God would not help her.

The preacher was a little different. His question was whether to choose church A or church B; both had asked him to serve. The preacher prayed and waited for God to provide a sign by shutting the door to either church A or church B, or by giving inner assurance that one was right and the other wrong, or by dropping a note down from heaven—anything that would reveal God's will in the matter. The preacher was willing to use his body wherever the Lord saw fit, but no word from heaven was forthcoming. Nothing.

The preacher went through several weeks of depression and tears and then realized that it didn't matter to God which church he served. At first he was shocked and felt abandoned by God. But after reeling for a while, he slowly came to realize that God was not concerned about where the preacher worked; God was concerned about the preacher. God wanted the man; where the man served was secondary.

When the preacher knew in his heart that he was truly willing to go wherever the Lord would send him and the Lord still remained silent, the only question was whether the man would like to go east or west. God could use him in either location. And a happy, peaceful preacher moved west.

We expect too little from ourselves.

Sometimes we avoid self-discipline because we expect a dramatic event to take place, something which will compel us to change our irresponsible behavior.

I often have folks in my office with "analysis paralysis." They want to dissect the problem, fuss about the problem, try to determine what caused the problem, and think of how awful it will be to try and solve the problem. They wear themselves out expending tons of mental energy trying to find a solution, but they resist taking a small step toward resolving the problem.

As a young wife I spent hours sitting in front of the TV berating myself because the TV was on and I should be getting work done instead of sitting there. How awfully sinful most of the programming was! How terrible I was for not studying the Bible more! What a bad influence all this was on my children! What a bad Christian I was! Why couldn't I break this habit? What method of control could I use? What guidelines could I follow? Maybe I needed to buy a new book on discipline. Perhaps I should cut the TV cord. I fussed and grumbled and beat myself with guilt.

One day while sitting there enjoying neither the program nor my guilty thoughts, bemoaning my lack of discipline, the Spirit seemed to say, "Well, you do have a hand." I couldn't deny that. I did have a hand. All of the muscles worked. I could flip the switch. Maybe I could not solve the problem forever and maybe I would turn the set back on in fifteen minutes . . . or even five . . . but I did have a hand. I could turn the TV off for that moment if I chose to yield my hand to do what I thought the Lord wanted.

I didn't like that idea. It was a lot easier to think about all the angles of the problem than to face the simple responsibility of the moment. But reluctantly, I yielded my hand as a living sacrifice and switched off the tube. By using that exercise repeatedly, within a month, the problem was solved.

We expect too much of ourselves.

In our effort to be a living sacrifice, some of us take on tasks so large that we constantly feel guilty for all we have left undone.

Our body is a marvelous creation, but it is only one body of one human, and it lives in a decaying world. There will always be more places to serve than ability, more needs to be met than resources, more people in pain than can be ministered to.

We hear the instruction of Jesus, "Go into all the world" (Mark 16:15), but one body can seldom do that. There are jobs and dishes, children and husbands, balancing the checkbook and taking time to brush our teeth. There is Aunt Jane that we promised to pray for and a meeting at the church at 7:00 (or was that 7:30?).

One feeble body that is limited to time and space and in need of sleep is a poor substitute to try and take over God's job for Him. The only way we can be living sacrifices and still remain sane is to remember that the Holy Trinity is not a quartet and we were not invited to join.

At times we feel the urgent call from the heart of God for a nation, a family, a church program, a ministry, and we long to be able to do it all and do it now as though the whole thing were our job. We try very hard to take the responsibility that God has reserved for His own, then wonder why we are tired!

We are living sacrifices, but God is running the show. It is God's responsibility to determine the ending, assign the parts, and direct. And at times He will direct us to sit still or to minister to ourselves and take care of our bodies so that they might serve Him more at a later date.

One of the most thrilling experiences for us as Christians can be the deep, inner knowledge that we have given our body as a living sacrifice to the Lord and that He has accepted it as holy (Rom. 12:1). If you have never had that experience, I encourage you to conduct an experiment this week. It will take only one day out of your life, but it could be a day that changes your life.

Spend one full day being aware of your body as a tool to be used as a living sacrifice for the Lord. When you are driving, look at your hands. When you walk, feel the muscles in your legs. Notice the temperature of the air on your skin and how your clothes feel on your body. Remember what water feels like. Smell. Taste. You may be surprised at how disconnected you have become from your own body. Take time to feel alive again.

Once you have connected with your body on an emotional level, consider one place you might yield that body as a sacrifice to the Lord. For instance, you might yield your tongue to say a kind word (or refrain from a harsh one). You might yield your hands to touch a child or yield your arms to vacuum the rug or yield your fingers to type a report. These may be ordinary things that you do all the time, but when they are done with an awareness that your body is a living sacrifice to God, even the most mundane chores can become a holy service and give you a new appreciation for the physical life which has been granted to you.

To complete this section on genetics, fill in the personal summation page. You might want to comment on what you felt as you worked certain exercises. Has the Lord shown you how you have rejected your body? Have you rejected your family? Have you spent too much time longing for a different world and not enough time becoming a living sacrifice where you live each day?

Personal Summation:

The following are the answers for the exercise on page 97.

1. False. Bodies are produced by design from our Creator, God (Gen. 5:1).

2. False. Ananias and Sapphira lost their physical lives because of sin (Acts 5:1–10).
   Sexual sins are often punished by physical ailments (Rom. 1:27).

3. True. Our body is the temple of God (1 Cor. 6:19–20).
   The Holy Spirit lives inside us (Rom. 8:11).
   Jesus said that He would be "in" His followers at a future date (John 14:20).

4. True. Paul's rhetorical question about differences between himself and Apollos included physical differences (1 Cor. 4:7).

5. False. Paul settled the argument that any one race or sex was superior to another (Gal. 3:28).

6. True. Flesh as we now know it will not be in heaven (1 Cor. 15:50–55).

7. False. The Bible confirms that things like cosmetics, ointments, and perfume are a delight and make us glad (Prov. 27:9).
   Jesus encouraged a good, clean physical appearance (Matt. 6:17).
   Paul assumed that mentally healthy people would naturally take care of their body (Eph. 5:29).

8. True. After the resurrection Jesus had a physical body He could enjoy (Luke 24:37–39).
   We are assured that after resurrection we, too, will have a body similar to the one He had (Phil. 3:21).

9. True. Paul kept his body disciplined as a method of making sure his whole life could be in submission to God (1 Cor. 9:27).

If we live to satisfy bodily appetites, we will die spiritually (Rom. 8:13).

Jesus taught that the spirit was more important than the body (Matt. 10:28).

10. False. Sexual appetites are good (Heb. 13:4).

Satisfying the appetite for food is encouraged (Neh. 8:10).

God is worshiped by feasting (Lev. 23:41).

11. False. Both body and spirit can glorify God (1 Cor. 6:20).

12. True. Harsh, unkind treatment of the body is a doctrine of false teachers and is useless in restraining sensual indulgences (Col. 2:23).

13. False. Many people were healed through Paul's work, but he had to leave his assistant Trophimus behind in Miletus when he became ill (2 Tim. 4:20).

James assures us that if illness is the result of sin, it can be broken through confession (James 5:14–16).

It is not an unusual thing for Christians to endure many different forms of suffering (1 Pet. 4:12).

14. False. We are given instructions not to "let" sin control us (Rom. 6:12).

If we resist Satan, he will flee (James 4:7).

15. False. Paul prayed that the whole spirit, soul, and body of his friends would be sanctified (1 Thess. 5:23).

16. False. If we can control our tongue, we can control our body (James 3:2).

17. True. We are instructed to present our bodies as instruments of God (Rom. 12:1–2).

The body is for the use of the Lord (1 Cor. 6:13).

P A R T
T H R E E

Environment,
Self Molded by
Time and
Circumstances

CHAPTER 7 ✣

Can I Trust My Memories?

I suppose that one of the things included in my genetic package is my tendency to be a bit of a ham. I love performing. This is especially true when I get an opportunity to sing.

In my family environment we were in church each Sunday, so my genetically given desire to sing expressed itself in church choirs and solos. One song I loved to sing was the old hymn by John T. Benson, "Precious Memories."

> Precious memories, how they linger
> how they ever flood my soul.
> In the stillness of the midnight
> precious memories, how they roll.
> Precious father, loving mother
> fly across the lonely years.
> And old home scenes of my childhood
> in fond memory appear.

I often sang that song with emotion, even shedding a tear or two, but I could not say that the words were true of my life. Yes, there had been good times, but there were the bad times too. And there were large lapses of memory. Years and years of total blank space. Was that normal? Was I normal? It bothered me to think about such things, so most of the time I simply ignored the subject and sang with a strange lump in my throat as I wondered about a childhood that had never been.

As I grew older, changed careers a couple of times, and ended up in an office talking to other folks about their memories, I found that the more I knew about this subject the less I was sure about. How the mind works to hold and process the experiences we encounter daily, forming them into memories that shape our lives, is a mystery to even the most astute scientist.

Psychologists, philosophers, linguists, neurosurgeons, neurobiologists, and computer scientists have all attempted to decipher how the brain holds and retrieves data, but until recently there has been little consensus among the experts as to how it is done.

One thing upon which all the scientists agree is this: We do remember things that happen around us and those memories impact who we are, how we act, and what we feel about ourselves and our world.

That is why this section on environment is necessary. We came into this world with a strong genetic package, but how that package finds expression in daily living will, to a large degree, be shaped by the world around us.

ALL THOSE TINY CHISELS

We bring a lot into this world. It is our personal baggage; our unique style and temperament and body. We are like no other person ever created. Even identical twins who share the exact same DNA will have separate minds and souls, ideas, reactions, and personalities. God makes no clones.

But that uniqueness is not the only part of this mysterious creation of God which we call "self." From the time we are born, life starts chipping away at us—forming us, shaping us, pushing us, grinding us, polishing us, breaking us—changing what *is* into what can be. The process will continue for as long as we live.

Self can be changed by the things in our environment because we remember. We know what happened to us. We remember the pain or the pleasure and we respond. This is how we learn rules of behavior and communication, how others should be treated, and how to approach others with our needs.

This chiseling effect life has on the body and soul is so pronounced and so well documented that at one time some leaders in the field of behavioral science asserted that they could produce an adult with whatever personality type they desired simply by controlling the events of early life, beginning with infancy.

They felt they could take a group of newborns and pick one to be a doctor and one to be a criminal and one to be passive and one to be assertive, then control the events that happened to the child and have each turn out according to design. This theory was never confirmed by research due to ethical considerations, but you can see how strongly they believed that past environment determines the future.

This deterministic view left the impression that people were basically biological machines and the brain, like a computer, would take data in and spit a certain kind of person out. Animal studies seemed to support these findings.

But the theories that looked so probable in the laboratory hit trouble when placed against reality. People didn't turn out to be as simple as mice. There was more to a brain than computer accuracy. There was not only a brain, there was a mind that perceived and responded according to more than cold data. One child growing up in the ghetto turned out to be a thief, while another under similar circumstances turned out to be president of a university. The same circumstances that turn one soul bitter create compassion in another. The behavioral scientists had no answer as to why this was so.

THE IMPACT
OF MEMORY

The events of our past do not predestine or control us, but they are part of us. How well we understand and accept those events can determine how firm of an identity we are able to establish and what that identity will be.

Most scientists do not believe the mind of a child is a total blank slate to be filled in by the events of life and shaped accordingly, but they do recognize the real impact of our past and its power to affect our present. A child born to an alcoholic father and a prostitute mother has much more to overcome than a child born into a loving, stable Christian home.

Our environment continues to influence us even after childhood. Our jobs, current family, health, church life, friends, children, and more are now shaping what we will be tomorrow and five years from now.

Because knowing and accepting our memories is an important part of knowing and accepting ourselves, we need to spend time examining our memories and learning a bit about how those memories were formed. I've included a list of resources at the end of this chapter if you wish to read further about memories or childhood development.

This section of the guidebook is devoted entirely to what you remember about what has happened to you. It is slightly different from the rest of the book for in this first chapter there are no exercises, but almost all of the next chapter will be written by you because it is about you—your history, your life. At the conclusion of this section, we will look at our environment from God's perspective.

THE STORAGE OF MEMORY

A popular song says that memories are "pressed between the pages of my mind," but scientists use less romantic terminology to express how memories are formed and stored. Yet neither the poet nor the researcher has managed to precisely illustrate how the mind works. This is because nothing with which we are currently familiar can accurately be compared to the amazing human brain. The three pounds of gray matter which God has graciously used to fill the hole beneath our skull is probably the most complex organism on earth. It has no equal.

At one time it was thought that comparing the brain to a huge computer might be an accurate illustration, but that idea has fallen out of favor lately because computers store each piece of data at a precise location. The brain, evidently, does not. Although some functions appear to be kept in various generalized locations, preciseness is another matter. This seems to be especially true where memory is concerned.

Recent efforts to illustrate how the brain works involve comparing each separate brain cell to a computer and visualizing each of these computers linked to several thousand other computers. Each separate computer shares information with some of the other computers but not all, and everything is tied together in systems and subsystems of varying sizes.

This leads us to conclude that even the mind of a severely retarded child can outperform anything NASA has created.

You have such a marvelous wonder just above your neck. In that small space you hold a vast amount of information including how to speak, how to drive a car, how to eat, and how to multiply. You also have your memories.

Memories may not always reside on a specific piece of brain tissue, but they do appear to occupy specific areas. They have been described as electrical imprinting that is stored over various fragments of nerve tissue. The imprinting becomes stronger each time the memory is recalled and asked to repeat itself to the conscious mind.

In the late 1950s a Canadian surgeon named Wilder Penfield stumbled upon some dramatic evidence while doing brain surgery on fully conscious patients diagnosed with epilepsy. He was using an electrode to stimulate various areas on the surface of the brain to try and find the specific source of the seizures. But to his surprise what Penfield found was that when he touched a particular spot, a patient might think he heard a sound or saw a flash of light. Some spots on the brain seemed to hold a memory of a melody while another would replay an incident from childhood. At the touch of an electrode, one woman felt that she was in her kitchen, listening to her boy playing outside; she worried at the sound of passing cars. A young man relived the experience of sitting at a baseball game, watching a child crawl under the fence to sneak inside. Each time Penfield stimulated the spot, the memory would play again.

Because of the work of Penfield and others, some experts believe that everything you have ever experienced or heard or seen is recorded somewhere in the vast systems of the brain. It is even suggested that the memories can be preverbal (stored before you were old enough to talk) and prenatal (before you were born).

All of that information, learning, experience, and thinking has gone into carving you bit by bit into who you are at this moment on this day. Working with our memories to find a new sense of who we are is not a problem of information storage but one of information retrieval. The memories are there, but bringing them to the surface and using them is another matter altogether.

THE ACCURACY OF MEMORY

I hit the wrong computer key the other day and erased almost a full chapter of this book. I groaned and grabbed the screen because I instantly knew what I had done, and as the data faded from sight I moaned, "How dare you! By now you ought to know what I want!" But it was no use. The command had been given, and the machine would follow through no matter what the cost to me and with no emotional response to my grief.

A computer chip stores a piece of data just as it is fed. It responds to commands exactly as they are received. But no matter how complex these machines are, they still cannot think. We could say that these machines have a brain but no mind.

We *do* have minds, and those minds are actively involved in memory storage and retrieval. We are not like a camera which records data. Our head is not a video input/output machine. We make judgments on what we see and continually move our data around so that it makes sense in our world and comfortably fits with other data we store.

This is why humans experience problems with memory which

never occur in the world of computers: memory discrepancy, memory blanks, and memory repression.

Memory Discrepancy

I have four adult children and six grandchildren scattered around the country and beyond. When we all manage to get together for a holiday, it is indeed special because of the distance that normally separates us. But there can be one discordant note that slips in on these peaceful, happy times. It most often occurs sometime after the last slice of turkey is picked apart and before the pie is served.

One of my kids will say, "Do you remember the time when . . ." and proceed to tell the story of a family experience. About that time a sibling will argue, "No, that wasn't how it happened. I distinctly remember . . ." and they will launch into their own, slightly different account of the event. By the time all four kids have given four different stories—none of which match my remembrance of the event—I am getting a little flustered, so I stand, tap a glass with a spoon to get their attention, and remind them that as a "shrink" I know what the problem is: Memories are recorded in the brain as they are perceived, not as the event actually occurred.

My speech doesn't settle the matter because they go on with their lively discussion, each insisting that their memory is right, and I end up with the same feelings I had when they were all in grammar school arguing over who took out the trash last.

You have probably experienced the same phenomenon in your family. This will especially be true if a year or so has lapsed between the time of the event and the time the stories are compared. You have also likely run into this phenomenon among your coworkers or classmates or with your husband. Whenever three people are involved in a single event, three slightly different memories of the event will be recorded.

This phenomenon is caused by more than just the fact that each person had a different vantage point and saw the scene from a different angle. It is more than the human tendency to shade the facts just a bit to make our side look better. A large part of the discrepancy will be created because we all fit current facts into our scheme of existing facts. Every moment of the present is given meaning as it relates to the past.

For example, pretend that I am five years old and in a car accident. I end up in the hospital with my father bending over my bed and Mama nowhere in sight. If I remember the times that Mama pushed me away and told me to be quiet because she was talking on the phone, I may believe that Mama is not there because she doesn't want to be. She likes the phone better than me.

The truth may be that Mama was in the accident, too, and no one has told me because they are involved with the tension and worry of the moment and are waiting to see if she will live before they tell me what happened. But that will not be my memory of the event, and it will not be the world to which I respond. My world and my mind tell me that Mama is on the phone and doesn't want to be bothered with my pain.

This same principle is active every day in far less dramatic ways. When we lose our car keys, we "remember" putting them in our purse because we always put them there. Acting on that memory, we assume that one of the kids took our keys, so we scold the kids. Later, we find the keys in the ignition, and we are embarrassed. At that point we are likely to utter something to the effect of, "I could have sworn I put those keys in my purse."

Our memory of a situation is recorded as we perceive it to be. If we think an event is frightening, it is recorded in the mind as frightening, no matter what the real danger might or might not be. If we believe we are abandoned, we *are* abandoned in our mind. If we believe we are safe and comfortable, we *are* safe and comfortable as far as memories are concerned.

This is why two siblings raised in the same home can grow up with two different perceptions of their parents: One feels loved and secure, but the other feels very abandoned and unloved.

Memory Blanks

Sometimes my clients worry because they cannot recall parts of their childhood, but such worry is often totally unfounded.

Absent memories do not necessarily mean that severe abuse took place during that time. Memory lapses or blanks have several explanations and are not unusual.

As stated earlier in this chapter, the brain probably records even the most mundane data on a daily basis. The brain's capacity for storage is almost limitless. Unless physical brain damage has occurred, the information is there. The problem is retrieving the information when we want it. Many things influence this retrieval process including natural ability, rehearsal, and triggers.

Natural Ability

The natural ability of some individuals to go back and pick out details of the past can be amazing. My son-in-law, Dustin, is like that. He has an uncanny ability to remember details of his past back to only a few months of age. My son, Billy, has a similar ability with numbers and can quote every car tag number, phone number, and address with which he has ever come in contact whether it is his own, a family member's, or a friend's. Yet I have to count on my fingers and toes and think for ten minutes before I can remember my own age.

Naturally talented people like these are fairly rare. Like those gifted people with photographic memories, they are simply endowed with the ability to access memories, probably part of their genetic heritage. But even these people bring a mind as well as a brain to the process of memory storage and retrieval, and their memories will have been stored as they were experienced, not necessarily as the events actually occurred.

For those of us who are not so gifted, accessing memories may be more difficult, but this does not mean that we are lacking in some way. It only means that we may be wired differently.

Rehearsal

Another reason for memory blanks is lack of practice in recalling memories. Like any other skill, memory recall gets easier as we exercise that skill. If you don't remember the fifth grade or can't remember the year and a half that the family lived in Oklahoma when you were eight, it may be because you have not had much practice accessing memories of those years. As you practice looking back at those years, some memories may begin to surface, memories which have drifted away from you over time.

Repeated rehearsal of memories will make those particular memories stronger and easier to access the next time you want them, and it will also make it easier to access other related memories.

Triggers

Memory blanks can also be caused by the absence of memory triggers. Our memories don't always just kick in when instructed to. We often need a key of some kind to unlock them. Things like family picture albums, talk around the dinner table, souvenirs, diaries, smells, names, colors, and architecture can be keys which help us remember.

If we have a habit of looking only at the present and ignoring these keys to the past, we will probably have greater memory lapse than someone who often relates things in the current world to things in the past.

In addition to lack of natural ability, lack of memory rehearsal, and the conscious ignoring of memory keys, lapses in memory can also be caused by unpleasant memories which the mind would rather not deal with. This is called *repression*.

Memory Repression

The idea of memory repression and an unconscious mind can be traced back to Sigmund Freud of Vienna in the late 1800s, and his classic psychoanalytic theory and technique. All therapists do not agree as to the importance of an unconscious mind and repressed memories or even that such things exist. But because it is obvious that all memory and all knowledge cannot be equally present to the conscious mind at the same time, it stands to reason that some must be stored elsewhere, and for the purpose of this book, we will call that somewhere the subconscious. This is the most hidden and least understood part of the mind, and it is here that repressed memories reside.

Evidence indicates that the vast majority of our memories cannot be recalled on command. The brain contains an ocean of memories, and we have the ability to access only a swimming pool's worth. This is not repression.

Lately I have come across many well-functioning adults who are stressed out because they fear they have repressed horrible memories that will someday spring on them unsuspected. Such worry is most often unfounded. As stated earlier, there are times when people think they were raised in healthy families but suddenly discover horrible memories of abuse, but those times are rare. So rare, in fact, that some professionals doubt their validity.

There are several kinds of repression and various professional theories as to its cause, but the child of God has no reason to fear any of them.

Repression refers to trauma. Something bad happens and the mind automatically files it away where it cannot be accessed so the conscious mind will not have to deal with it. These events, like all others, are received and recorded in the mind as they are perceived, not necessarily as they actually occurred.

Repression most often happens in the traumatic drama of an instant, like a car wreck or house fire. The memory loss can be complete or partial, but it usually returns within a few hours, days, or weeks.

Repression also occurs when emotion is separated from event. Most often the event is remembered, but the emotion—both past emotion and current feeling about the event—is not. I suspect it can also be that the event is forgotten and only the emotion is remembered such as in Post Traumatic Stress Disorder, but that is debatable.

It is far more rare for both the emotion and the event to be forgotten. This seems to be even more unlikely if the traumatic event was repeated over a long period of time. If the event was repeated over time (such as in repeated child abuse), some experts feel that it cannot be repressed, but other, equally qualified professionals disagree. Because this phenomenon is rare, it is difficult to prove.

As I studied the phenomenon of repressed memories I agreed first with one expert then changed my mind and agreed with a different view—until the day the subject became personal and I found myself moving through my own private twilight zone.

I tell the story here because it so clearly illustrates the fact that memories are stored according to perception and that keys can unlock memories. It also demonstrates the power repressed memories can have in our lives.

THE MEMORY THAT NEVER WAS

I had a little time off and was holed up in my apartment for a couple of days studying Multiple Personality Disorder and ritual abuse. The text I was reading was rather graphic, but studying such things is not unusual in my business. Looking at the down side of life is something counselors do every work day, but for some reason this study stirred something in me that I couldn't explain and did not like.

I would study for an hour or two; my nerves would become as tight as fiddle strings. I was restless, frightened perhaps, or maybe I should say apprehensive.

The next day I found I had no appetite and the thought of meat made me sick, but I knew I was not physically ill. What was going on? *Come on,* I told myself. *This is your profession. What is happening to you?* I had no idea.

By the third day I called my landlady. "Judy, I have either got to go to the mall and buy clothes I can't afford, or eat this whole bag of Oreo cookies, or go for a walk and talk to somebody sane for an hour. Will you walk with me?"

We walked and she patiently listened to me unload, but this did not relieve my uncomfortable feelings and I still had no idea what was going on inside me.

The next morning I was in that mental state between sleep and consciousness when slowly, like a balloon rising gently, a memory drifted into the light from somewhere deep inside a dark spot of my soul. I remembered my rabbit.

I could clearly remember being eight or nine years old and seated at the supper table. Mama and Daddy were arguing and my stomach was sick. Daddy had killed my pet rabbit and fried it. A large chunk of it was on my plate, and I was being scolded for not eating. After all, the others had worked so hard to provide for me.

The memory explained several symptoms that I had all my adult life. Why I sometimes had an unexplained aversion to meat. Why I avoided the section of the market where game meat was displayed for sale. Why, when my children were young, I could insist that they eat their vegetables or drink their milk but never could force myself to insist they eat meat.

But that is not the end of the story. I had also been doing some study on memory reliability. This was a true memory, but did it really happen? There could be no question that this event was stored deep inside my mind and it had influenced my life, but how did it line up with the reality that others were experiencing at that time?

I wanted to find some way to validate this traumatic event in my life, and after some thought I decided to approach my mother for her view of the situation. Why did she let Daddy get away with such cruelty? Many years had passed since my childhood, and my mother had changed. Dad was dead, but the strength Mama had always exhibited had matured her into one of the godliest women I had ever known. I thought it would be safe to broach such a delicate subject with her.

I was surprised at how quickly Mama bristled when I first related the memory to her. But after I assured her that I was not looking to condemn or blame, but only for an explanation to give me a better understanding of my own feelings, she quietly thought about it for a moment. Then she said, "In the first place, you never had a pet rabbit."

"OK, Mom," I said. "Your ability to judge the situation as a young mother was probably better than mine as an eight year old. But how do you explain the memory? Were there ever any rabbits in my life?"

"Only one that I remember. We lived in Torrance when you were about that age, and the man next door raised rabbits as a sideline business."

As the afternoon wore on, I was able to piece together how my memory could be true as I experienced it and yet not true according to reality.

The man next door not only had rabbits but also a son who was my best friend. I knew I would grow up someday and marry Butch Hammonds. It is likely that Butch "gave" me one of the many caged rabbits that lived at the back of his yard. I could have fed it and petted it through the cage and easily "had" a pet rabbit. Butch's father would occasionally slaughter the adult rabbits and sell the hides.

When the fact that my rabbit showed up missing with blood on the ground combined with the heated argument between Mom and Dad and the stress of some abuse that I was enduring at the time, my eyes looked at the plate of meat at supper that night and I "knew" my dad had killed my rabbit and was going to force me to eat it.

That memory was so traumatic that it was pushed inside a locked closet in my brain, hurting me so deeply that it was impossible to keep it totally hidden; therefore, I continued to experience an aversion to meat well into my adult years. Because I was studying case histories of ritual abuse victims, some of which involved the eating process, the hidden memory began to come alive and finally surfaced. My memory was true. The damage was true. But it did not really happen as I remembered.

CAN I TRUST MY MIND?

In my effort to clarify one side of an issue, I fear that I may have overstated my case. I do not want you to feel that the mind cannot be trusted or that memories are unreliable tools for fostering personal growth and understanding.

While memories may be stored as they are perceived, they are put together with the building blocks of the real world. People who are not psychotic do not normally remember events that have no basis in reality.

The most important reason that we should trust our memories is because no matter what details may have been rearranged or overlooked, perception is where we live and it is that level to which we must respond.

For instance, if I perceived my parents as cold and uncaring because they were never there when I needed them, my obligation to forgive and work past my bitterness and learn to trust does not change according to the reality that others may have been experiencing.

It does not matter whether they really loved me but were so involved with financial crises that they had little time and energy to express the love; it does not matter whether my sister or brother experienced them as I did; neither does it matter if it were twice as bad as I thought and they in truth hated me. None of this would change my obligation to accept the environment God has allowed to come into my life.

Seeing the situation from another's viewpoint, searching for the truth of reality, and understanding why another person responded as they did are all important, but they do not help me understand who I am and how my memories have shaped me.

The chisel that came against our life to shape and change us is the memory as we perceive it to be. The understanding of self and the acceptance of self is to be found at that level. The other issues are important and affect how we establish relationships with others, but the subject of this guidebook is our relationship with our self.

It is very easy to get stuck concentrating on how things "really" were and arguing with others over why our memories and feelings are justified and correct. We would be much better off if we practiced the following three steps:

Step One:

Accept our personal feelings and memories at face value just as they are and stop insisting on outside validation before we move responsibly to resolve these things inside ourselves.

Step Two:

Allow others to hold their own memories and feelings without trying to convince them why they are wrong or how they should feel.

Step Three:

Seek to understand the reality of events as God sees them. Objective reality is important for understanding ourselves and others and our world. It is also occasionally important to communicate reality to another, but this step *must* follow the other two.

MEMORY JOGGERS

Now I would like to introduce you to some "memory joggers" which can help you to release your inaccessible memories. These processes work well for truly repressed memories, but they also work for that vast storehouse that we simply can't access due to lack of practice or lack of natural talent.

As you work on the next chapter, you may want to try one or more of these methods for calling out your past. Each is simple and self-explanatory. You may find that one is more helpful to you than the others, so feel free to experiment.

Interviewing

If there is a certain blank spot in your childhood, one of the best ways to learn about it is to simply ask. It amazes me how little communication there is in most families. Your brothers and sisters or parents can offer a world of information. If you don't remember yourself as a preschooler, ask Aunt Jane to tell you what she remembers. You don't have to believe everything others say, but listening to their perceptions of your life at that age may trigger a memory of your own, or you may find out how your life was impacted by a bitter person like Aunt Jane!

Forced Writing

The brain does not like to be pushed, but sometimes it does its best work that way. Brainstorming is a technique which many businesses use to generate new ideas when the best minds are "stuck." Forced writing works the same way.

To try a round of forced writing all you need is paper, pencil, and a clock. First, remove all distractions: take the phone off the hook, put the kids to bed, and turn off the TV. Then set the clock for twenty minutes and start writing about your subject.

The only rule is that you must keep writing. Don't let the pencil stop. If you can't think of a memory, write about the fact that you can't think. If you feel self-conscious doing that exercise, write about feeling self-conscious. Don't check your spelling. Don't worry about sentence structure. Don't get upset if you stray from your original subject. Just keep writing, that is all.

When the alarm goes off, stop. Later, go back and read what you have written. You may be surprised at what the mind jars loose when pushed.

Physical Triggers

Your life is probably recorded in many different places. All of these physical records can remind you of memories and feelings. Family picture albums are a good source of memories, but so are old diaries that you have written, the baby book your mother kept, school yearbooks, and church or school records. Even legal documents such as adoption records, court proceedings, and marriage licenses tell about you and the family of which you were a part.

Reviewing these records can increase your awareness of history and identity.

Art

Artistic expression is a major part of many psychiatric hospital programs and is often used to help individuals get in touch with memories. It can also release feelings associated with those memories. There are several forms of artistic expression, but one of the most common is the collage.

To produce a therapeutic collage, begin by choosing a subject (your high school years, your feelings toward your dad, an autobiographical sketch of your life, etc.). Then spend a couple of weeks collecting odds and ends from magazines or newspapers that remind you of that subject. Good sources for pictures are magazines about children (such as *Parents Magazine*) and religious publications. Try to collect a good stack of twenty to fifty pictures.

After you have selected your pictures, choose a time when you will not be disturbed and start to experiment with the pictures, arranging them on a large sheet of paper. You may find that once you start, the project takes on a life of its own and things just seem to fit or be out of place by their own accord. Draw pictures if you like, use background colors, or use family snapshots. There are no rules; just put it together until it feels right.

Once you have completed the project, find a friend you can trust and share the collage. Talk your way through all the pictures, and tell how they relate to the subject you are expressing.

Relaxation

Chasing a memory can be like trying to catch a pigeon in the park. The thing is oh, so close, but when you reach out to lay your hand on it, the object backs away. The harder you chase it, the faster it runs. This is why an important part of memory retrieval is often the talent of relaxation.

Working on the next chapter may take some time; in fact, it may take longer than the rest of this guide put together. That is OK. Rest and let it happen naturally.

You may think there is nothing else to write about a particular stage of your life, then three days later while you're preparing dinner, a memory that is very significant may surface. If is often at the times when we are between sleep and wakefulness or doing mundane, repetitious tasks that memories will peek around the corner.

As you begin the next chapter, ask God to bring to mind those parts of your past that you may have rejected and then trust Him to do that for you. Nothing is going to come to light that He can't handle. Discovering how you have been shaped by your environment can be an exciting adventure. *This is your life. Embrace it!*

S. R. Ambron and N. Salkind, *Child Development* (New York: Holt, Rinehart and Winston, 1981), 134–135.

G. Craig, *Human Development* (Englewood Cliffs, NJ: Prentice-Hall, 1986), 142–152.

G. Johnson, *In the Palaces of Memory* (New York: Alfred A. Knopf, 1991).

K. Leman and R. Carlson, *Unlocking the Secrets of Your Childhood Memories* (Nashville: Thomas Nelson, 1989).

H. Wakefield and R. Underwager, *Magic, Mischief, and Memories: Remembering Repressed Abuse* (Northfield, MN: Institute for Psychological Therapies).

CHAPTER 8

My Life's Story

Many theorists have developed various ways of looking at childhood and the entire life experience by dividing it into stages. This stage thinking has permeated our popular culture as well. It is where exasperated parents get the phrase, "Oh, he is just going through a stage, it will pass." We think of life as steps, and when one is gone, another is on the threshold.

Erik Erikson, a developmentalist theoretician and a student of Freud, eventually went his own way and developed what is known as a psychosocial view of human development. He looked at life as a whole and felt people naturally passed through eight stages from birth to death. At each stage the person has a specific task to learn, and no future stage can be processed as it should unless the one before it has been truly mastered. All the tasks are presented as polarized statements: basic trust vs. mistrust; autonomy vs. shame and doubt; initiative vs. guilt; industry vs. inferiority; identity vs. role confusion; intimacy vs. isolation; generativity vs. stagnation; and integrity vs. despair.

Although these stages are attached to ages, they should not be thought of as rigid states fixed to specific times. We are learning trust, identity, intimacy our whole lives. But our first encounters with these aspects usually happens in the approximate time Erikson proposed, and that first encounter often sets the tone for what follows later. Lack of success at that time can make relearning the issue at a future stage more difficult.

Erikson's theory of stages, like other psychological data, are not biblical and thus not infallible, but they can be a useful tool. I have decided to use this tool to shape a framework on which you can hang your memories and other environmental information.

In this chapter, each of the eight stages is briefly discussed along with the developmental challenges to be mastered. You will be asked to recall your personal experience of each.

I have tried to provide a reasonable amount of space for recording what may be on your heart. If you feel the need to go into a lot of detail, do not limit yourself to the space provided in this guidebook. You may want to purchase a ring binder and divide it into eight sections. That way, additional memories can be added as they come up simply by adding more pages where needed. You can use the notebook method to write an entire detailed autobiography and even include letters and mementoes, but I would encourage you to keep such an ambitious project separate from the work of this guidebook.

If you are working with a separate, more extensive script, you can transfer what you consider most significant to the guidebook so that all your work on personal identity will be in this one volume.

You need not restrict your work in any way. Good memories and bad ones; information about yourself and stories others have told you; things you suspect and things that you know can all be included. The good parts will provide a positive counterbalance to those parts that may be embarrassing, painful, or uncomfortable. By looking at the negative memories, you may find issues to be resolved, wounds that need God's healing touch. Be diligent and open to the process of discovering who you are and where you came from.

STAGE ONE:
EARLY INFANCY
(BIRTH–1 YEAR)

One thing you know for certain is that you were born. Where, to whom, your parents' ages, social conditions at the time, and your health are all important. These are parts of your identity, and they affect how you view yourself and your world.

What do you remember being told about yourself at this stage of life? Not many people have memories of this stage, but some do. Were you told if your birth was planned or unplanned? What would you guess?

Erikson taught that the major task learned at this very early age was the task of basic trust versus mistrust. If you cried and were fed, it is likely that you learned that your needs could be met and the world was a fairly safe place to be. If you were in pain a lot or had many needs that went unmet, you probably saw the world as unsafe and felt that the people in it could not be trusted.

Write what you know, things you were told or assumed, and any memories that you have from birth to one year. Numbering each separate memory or issue may make it easier to reference your work later.

_____

_____

_____

_____

_____

_____

_____

_____

_____

_____

_____

_____

_____

_____

_____

_____

_____

_____

_____

_____

_____

_____

_____

STAGE TWO: LATER INFANCY (1–3 YEARS)

If a brother or sister was born during this stage, you had to share your parents' attention with the newcomer. You were still learning trust, but the most basic elements of that task were probably set in your mind.

During this second stage, you were no longer totally helpless. You were beginning to experience a little control of your world at the toddler stage. You mastered many of the basic skills of life, such as walking, feeding yourself, speaking, and that most important skill of all, potty training.

Erikson felt the major task of this stage was the struggle for autonomy against shame and doubt. As you demonstrated your independence with these new skills, were you applauded for your efforts or shamed? If you reached for the milk to feed yourself and spilled it, were you taught that it was good to reach anyway, or were you shamed for your clumsiness and punished for your effort to be independent?

Based on what you know about your family and stories of your parents' lives and struggles at that time, what do you think your world would have been like? If you have true memories of this age, write about them and be sure to include any emotions you remember that surround the memories.

_____
_____
_____
_____
_____
_____
_____
_____
_____
_____
_____
_____
_____
_____
_____
_____
_____
_____
_____
_____
_____

STAGE THREE: EARLY CHILDHOOD (4-5 YEARS)

The social circle widens for most children about this time. Before this age, children may play side by side, but they almost never play together. A pair of two-year-olds will play with a pile of toys, but each will have her own toy and each will be occupied with her own thoughts and actions. A pair of five-year-olds may play together by throwing a ball back and forth or building a joint block project.

Children at this age have a new ability to observe themselves and others. They also learn that they are expected to control themselves. This brings them to a dilemma: They are experiencing themselves as more powerful than ever before, but they are beginning to realize that they must control their own behavior, and they will feel guilty if they fail to do so. Erikson felt the primary task of a child at this stage was the struggle to resolve the power of initiation versus guilt for doing the wrong thing.

Whether you remember it or not, during this stage you began to experience feelings of guilt whenever your behavior was inappropriate. You also began to recognize that your actions produced certain consequences.

As you record your facts and memories, think of how these experiences might have shaped you. What did they tell you about your world? What did they tell you about yourself?

_____

_____

_____

_____

_____

_____

_____

STAGE FOUR: MIDDLE CHILDHOOD (6–11 YEARS)

This is the age of collections, hobbies, projects, and clubs. The boys don't like the girls, and the girls sometimes don't like the boys—well, almost don't like them anyway.

You probably have some clear memories of this age. Your social structure widened dramatically, and friends were very important. School occupied much of your time and energy, but home and family still represented security to you. Your position on the social ladder was understood by both you and your peers.

Erikson thought the major task of this life stage was the struggle of industry versus inferiority. At this age children want to try new things, and they feel much relief and pleasure in pleasing and accomplishing. But there is a potential danger at this stage: What we do can be measured against what others can accomplish. We will repeatedly have experiences like our model car not winning a ribbon in the contest or not being chosen for the team. We will give the wrong answer or stumble when we try to read out loud and be teased by fellow classmates.

If home was a safe and accepting place for you at this stage, you had a shelter that could make the act of industry and trying to reach worth the risk of feeling inferior when those efforts were judged as less than adequate by the outside world. But if home was not a safe place of acceptance, you may not have felt free to reach; in fact, you may have withdrawn and closed off a part of yourself.

There are many ways a family can go wrong, but some of the patterns that we frequently see are: (1) A highly critical parent who always finds fault in a project or report card; (2) A parent who fails to praise or appears unconcerned with a child's accomplishments; (3) A parent who lives vicariously through the child and is emotionally involved with each success and failure as though it were their life, not the child's; and (4) An upside-down family where the parents are immature and push responsibility on the child that should be borne by the adult. Sometimes the child will be responsible for the care and feeding of younger siblings, or household chores that would normally fall to the adult are pushed on the child, or the child becomes an emotional crutch, made to listen to the problems of the parent. These situations create stress for the child, effectively stealing away her happiness and innocence.

This stage is such an active and important stage of life that a little extra room has been added for your autobiographical sketch. If you have any memories, good or bad, that are especially strong, be sure to include them even if you are not certain at this point how they fit into the overall picture.

STAGE FIVE: PUBERTY AND ADOLESCENCE (12–20 YEARS)

Rapid changes take place in the teen years—physical, psychological, emotional, spiritual, and relational changes.

In this stage the mind starts stretching and seriously contemplating such abstract ideas as, Where is the end of space? and, What good is a government? and, Why should I go to church? This is called formal operational thought, and it is first experienced somewhere in the early to mid-teens. This is like a new door opening in the mind that was never there before. In these years a true self-identity is formed for the first time. In fact, Erikson said that the central task of these years would be identity versus role confusion.

The identity process begins as the teen pulls away from seeking total identity in the family. But being immature and lacking a firm identity of their own, they often begin to substitute peer and group identity for a genuine identity of self as an individual. They pick a group and dress like, talk like, and think like that group.

At this point, identity is a pseudo front that the teen is trying on to see how it fits. The tragedy is that the teen sees himself as invincible and does not realize the danger created by this identity switching and experimentation.

Statistically, the teen years are very dangerous. Teens are more likely to die in an accident, more likely to commit suicide, more likely to be arrested, more likely to be committed to a psychiatric hospital, and more likely to become addicted to drugs. Decisions made during this stage may cause permanent damage to the individual.

What were your teen years like? Do you remember certain clothes that identified you with a particular group? Did you try on other identities, experimenting with drugs, alcohol, or sex?

What were your feelings as you left home? What are the memories that come most clearly to mind? What were your questions about God and morality and justice? Were you so busy trying to hold a "good girl" front before other people that you never found the real you on the inside?

If you married during your teen years, you may want to record only the years before marriage in this section.

_____
_____
_____
_____
_____
_____
_____
_____
_____
_____
_____
_____
_____
_____
_____
_____
_____
_____
_____
_____
_____
_____
_____
_____

_____

_____

_____

_____

_____

_____

_____

_____

_____

_____

_____

_____

_____

_____

_____

_____

_____

STAGE SIX: EARLY ADULTHOOD (20–30 YEARS)

Erikson could have called these the searching years, but instead he said they were the years when the central task was intimacy versus isolation. Most people marry during these years, and even those who do not are faced with the task of finding someone to whom they can relate on a soul-to-soul level.

God has created our hearts with a need to reach out. We desire to touch and be touched by another. We need another person who enjoys our presence and lights up when we come near. Often we dream that such a need will be met in marriage, and we are disappointed if it is not.

In these years we learn how to be an individual and yet be vulnerable and intimately involved with others. Ideally, we learn how to be responsible in our relationships, giving and receiving in a mutually fulfilling way.

You will likely have more memories of these years than can be recorded in the space allowed. Think back and choose those that seem most significant. Record both facts and your feelings about those facts. What were your major hurts? What lessons, if any, can you identify as clearly being taught by the Lord?

It might be worthwhile to spend a little time talking with your husband or your family to get a view of your life from their perspective. What did they see happening to you? Have they seen changes in you, good or bad, as those years rolled across your life?

_____

_____

_____

_____

_____

_____

_____

_____

_____

_____

_____

_____

_____

_____

_____

_____

_____

_____

_____

_____

_____

_____

_____

_____

_____

STAGE SEVEN: MIDDLE ADULTHOOD (30–40 YEARS)

Erikson saw the challenge of these years as generativity versus stagnation. We either give way to the status quo and stop growing as individuals, or we are motivated to keep life fresh and accept new challenges. This motivation comes from within, not from others. We either become active participants (generativity), or we become passive observers, contented with whatever happens (stagnation).

Unfortunately, in our society many couples divorce during these years. Marriages also grow stale in these years, and careers level off or lose their challenge. Of course, this is not true of everyone, but it is mentioned here to cause you to think about the emotions and events in your environment and to consider how they may have affected your development.

_____

_____

_____

_____

_____

_____

_____

_____

_____

_____

_____

_____

_____

_____

_____

_____

_____

_____

_____

_____

_____

_____

_____

_____

_____

_____

_____

_____

_____

_____

_____

_____

_____

_____

_____

_____

_____

_____

_____

_____

STAGE EIGHT:
LATE
ADULTHOOD
(41+ YEARS)

The existential issues (who am I, where am I going, etc.) that were first confronted in the teen years, often seem less important during the early and middle years of adult life. We are so busy with living day to day that the major questions of life almost go underground.

In the last half of life, these questions surface once again with new urgency. Erikson called this stage integrity versus despair. If we find personal answers to those big questions, an inner dignity that even death cannot shake is ours. Otherwise, we may come to view our lives as meaningless, with no purpose, logic, or goal; the despair of the emptiness is all that is left. For the Christian, this stage of life should be the culmination of a life lived in faith. In those earlier stages, we learned the Christian response to life's challenges, but by this stage we have experienced many of those truths firsthand. Now they become a part of us, unshakable and rock solid.

Remember, the stages of life development presented here have listed the common ages at which certain issues are first experienced. Many of you may feel that you have established the dignity and security of purpose much earlier in life. But as I approach my own fiftieth birthday and look back over my shoulder, I believe some things in life are only won by time. For myself, the brash assurance of my twenties cannot match the settled faith of today.

If you are past forty-one, you can now write your memories of the events in this last stage. If you are younger, but believe life has meaning and purpose is beyond doubt, write about why you feel as you do and when you came to experience these truths emotionally.

_____

_____

_____

_____

_____

_____

_____

_____

_____

_____

_____

_____

_____

_____

_____

_____

_____

_____

_____

_____

_____

_____

_____

_____

WHY DID I PICK THAT MEMORY?

What makes certain memories quickly come to the consciousness and others not? Why do we sometimes have strong emotional attachment to memories which seem to be inconsequential?

Two reasons are that we have a tendency to remember strongly impressed, dramatic moments, and that we can quickly recall the things we often rehearse, but Kevin Leman and Randy Carlson in their book, _Unlocking the Secrets of Your Childhood Memories_ (Nashville: Thomas Nelson, 1989), have another theory to add to the list. They call it "Creative Consistency."

Creative Consistency basically means that you will draw to conscious memory those things that are consistent with your current view of life. If you view yourself as a victim of circumstance, your earliest memories will likely be those of victimization even if that victimization is your big brother pounding you before taking a toy from you. I have found in counseling married couples that I can indeed get quickly to the central issues of the marriage and understand my clients' views of life by asking them to relate their early memories.

Recently when a new couple made their first trip to my office,

I asked them to recall memories. The man related three rather humorous stories of pranks he had pulled as a kid or scrapes he had been in, and each time he told a story, I noticed that he was rescued from his daring by a woman.

When the wife related her memories, I noticed that she was always alone and never once mentioned being involved in any way with another human even though she related several clear memories.

I was not surprised when she said the central issue of the marriage problem was his irresponsibility and refusal to take life seriously, and his complaint was her coldness and sexual distance.

After reading Leman and Carlson's book I thought about my own early memories. There was only one. I was around age six and probably had just started first grade. I was standing at the edge of the school yard observing the other children as they played. I was not sad or lonely. I was just curious and interested in what the others did and how they responded to each other. I also wanted to know and thoroughly understand the rules of the playground before I risked joining. I would never have dared to run to the sandbox until I was sure that it was not only OK for children to do that, but it was OK for *me* to do that. Now, forty-three years later, I am still very much an observer, curious and interested, but slow to join in and always considering the importance of the rules and the approval of others.

Using the idea of creative consistency, think back on the earliest memories you have recorded. Especially remember how you felt, what emotions were involved.

Do these emotions and responses seem consistent with who you are and how you view life today? Why or why not?

As discussed in the previous chapter, we have been shaped by our environment. The expression of our natural genetic heritage will be restricted or encouraged by life and by those around us. The things that have happened to us and our responses to those events have taught us about life and ourselves.

To help you discover how your environment may have shaped you, read the following list and put a check mark by those statements which apply to you. Continue the exercise by filling in your own ideas about what your environment taught you.

1. ☐ When demands were made that I could not fill, I learned to doubt myself and my decisions.

2. ☐ When I began to receive approval from others outside the family, I learned to look for my good feelings there, not at home.

3. ☐ When we moved frequently, I learned that it was safer not to make friends; that way, leaving would not be so painful.

4. ☐ When I was not allowed to show emotion, I learned to hide my emotions or express them in only negative ways.

5. ☐ When I was told I had to go to church, I learned to see the importance of God in my life.

6. ☐ When I was forced to go to church, I learned to hate everything to do with organized religion.

7. ☐ When I saw adults around me solve problems by screaming, I learned to solve my problems by screaming.

8. ☐ When I was frightened and intimidated by adults who were angry and out of control, I learned to fear anger in myself and others.

9. ☐ When _____
   I learned _____
   _____ .

10. ☐ When _____
    I learned _____
    _____ .

11. ☐ When _____
    I learned _____
    _____ .

12. ☐ When _____
    I learned _____
    _____ .

13. ☐ When _____
    I learned _____
    _____ .

14. ☐ When _____
    I learned _____
    _____ .

15. ☐ When _____
    I learned _____
    _____ .

WHAT I CAN CHANGE

We cannot change our past environment anymore than we can change our genetic heritage, but we can change how we react today. We can choose a different future. If we never had an opportunity for an education, we can choose to go to school now even if we are well into the adult years. If we were scarred or robbed by others, we can learn to accept what happened and allow God to heal our wounds.

You can begin the process of accepting your past and putting it to rest. Start by filling out the personal summation page, writing about those things that have hurt you and how they may have affected your relationships with others and your relationship with yourself. Talk about the feelings you remember and how they may have impacted your life in positive or negative ways. Explain your desires for a different future.

 Personal Summation:

Personal Summation:

CHAPTER 9 ❧

Why Did God Allow My Circumstance?

I will never forget the look on her face. It was not condemnation or anger. She had passed those stages. It was not even hopelessness. Her soft brown eyes looked wounded and puzzled and she reminded me of a hunted deer. Why had God not answered her prayer? That was all she wanted to know.

Chelsey had come from a home with more distance and emptiness than love. The only time she felt wanted was during the summers when she spent time with her grandparents.

Grandma and Grandpa lived in a small town with a little church nearby, and every Sunday they dressed Chelsey in her best and the family went to church together. At church, Chelsey learned about Jesus who wanted to be a friend to little children. Although she was only nine years old, Chelsey understood the stories and understood about her own sin. She gave her heart to Jesus and was baptized one summer.

The Sunday school teacher had told her that Jesus was strong and that He would be her protector and helper; the mighty God of all the universe would hear and answer her prayers. That sounded very good to Chelsey because she had a secret problem and she needed protection.

Her summers with Grandma and Grandpa were ideal except for one thing. Her Grandpa seemed to be two different men. One man was good and kind and smiled all the time, but the other man forced her to keep secrets and sometimes hurt her during the night. She was confused and did not know what to do. So one night she prayed, and she asked her new friend Jesus if He would stop Grandpa from coming into her room.

Chelsey lay awake and watched the door. Maybe Jesus could fix it. Maybe Jesus would not let Grandpa come. Then after everyone else was asleep, she saw the door open as it had so many times before. An hour later, alone once again, she was curled in the corner crying silently, afraid to go back to the warm bed, remembering what always happened there.

Now, as a thirty-year-old woman, Chelsey sat in my office with her doe-like eyes and asked, "Why didn't Jesus stop Grandpa?"

THE QUESTION OF THE AGES

Why does God allow such pain? How can a good God let bad things happen in this world? I have asked this question more than a few times. And I don't believe I have ever met a mature saint that hasn't spent time wrestling with God over this very issue.

"My God! Where are You when I need You?" This has been the heart cry of millions. It was also the cry of the Psalmist (Pss. 22:1; 22:19; 27:9; 38:21; 71:12). Even Jesus asked that question (Matt. 27:46; Mark 15:34).

You, too, have probably asked that question at least a few times in your life, and I wish I could tell you that reading the rest of this book would totally resolve the puzzle for you, but that is not true. Your journey through life is a personal one, and so are some of the answers to life. While academic rationale, Bible study, and listening to testimonies of others can be of great benefit, the final answer has to be taken by faith. That is a bridge each person must cross alone.

However, I can share with you how I have been able to embrace the things I don't like or don't understand about myself, my life, and my God. I hope that by sharing with an honest heart and by the work of the Holy Spirit, you can be helped too.

Personally, I found a lot of peace when I came to see three things: (1) The good and bad of my life is normal, not something to be avoided; (2) God takes full responsibility for both the evil and the good; and (3) Everything has a purpose. God is always in control.

Think back over your answers to the questions in the genetic and environment sections of this guidebook. You can probably identify specific areas where you have chosen to reject rather than experience the pain of accepting reality. You may have wondered why God allowed this painful reality in your life. Choose three of the most difficult realities and write them in the form of questions to God.

1. _____

_____

_____

2. _____

_____

_____

3. _____

_____

_____

LIFE IS A MIXTURE OF GOOD AND EVIL

The world as we know it did not start with creation. It started with what is sometimes called the Fall, when Adam and Eve disobeyed God. If it has been a while since you read this account, go back to the third chapter of Genesis and refresh your memory because the next few paragraphs and exercises will be quite detailed.

In the garden of Eden God created two trees—the Tree of Knowledge of Good and Evil and the Tree of Life. The fruit of each tree was designed to do what the name implied. One would supply the knowledge of good and evil and the other would supply eternal life.

Too often we read the name of the first tree and mentally substitute *righteousness* and *unrighteousness* for the terms *good* and *evil*. But that is not what the terms mean, and that is not what the tree was designed to give.

The word *good* means everything good. If it is happy; if it smells pleasant; if it is pretty; if it tastes good; if it has a purpose; if it gives joy—it could be described as *good*. The Bible uses this word to refer to healthy stocks of ripe corn (Gen. 41:5).

Evil does not mean unrighteousness. It is the same word used in Jeremiah 24:3, where in a vision God asked Jeremiah what he saw and Jeremiah replied, "Figs; the good figs, very good; and the evil, very evil, that cannot be eaten, they are so evil" (KJV). The word *evil* as involved in the tree's name includes everything bad, unwanted, rotten, stinking, and painful. Evil is to be rejected.

The word *knowledge* in the name is not just an abstract, academic knowledge. It is an experiential, hands-on involvement with the subject matter, as when used in the verse, "Adam knew Eve his wife, and she conceived" (Gen. 4:1).

Thus, when Eve chose the wisdom to be granted by the Tree of Knowledge of Good and Evil, she was expressing a desire to experience a life which included a mixture of pain and pleasure, good and bad, joy and sorrow. At that time she had never experienced pain or sorrow, so she made her choice without much ability to accurately judge what those times would really be like. Perhaps that is why Paul said that Eve was "deceived" (1 Tim. 2:14).

At the very moment when Adam and Eve disobeyed God, life became a mixture of good and evil for all who would follow. Never would there be anything or anyone totally good (except Christ) and all would need redemption.

But somehow this obvious fact escapes us when we are in pain. We become surprised to find this unwanted thing in our life. Pain is an insult. How dare life treat us this way!

When we look back at a painful or seemingly unfair time, our first thought can often be *Why me?* That question indicates two things. First, it shows our desire for control. If we can find out what we did to deserve the problem, we can quit doing it and make the problem go away! Second, it demonstrates our amazing ability to deal with life illogically. We know that good and bad things happen in this life, but we are surprised when the bad touches us personally.

Peter encouraged Christians, "Beloved, do not think it strange concerning the fiery trial which is to try you, as though some strange thing happened to you" (1 Pet. 4:12). It was as though the apostle was a bit surprised that the people did not accept the presence of pain in their lives. Peter regarded pain as a normal part of life for both Christian and non-Christian. But for the Christian, it had an added dimension and reward that the unbeliever could never know (1 Pet. 4:13–17).

Look up 1 Peter 4:12–19 and complete the following.

1. We should not be surprised at our painful experience, but instead

2. If we bear the name of Christ (Christian) and we are insulted, then

3. If we suffer, it should not be because

4. But if we are innocent and we suffer, we should never be

5. If we suffer because we have sinned, we should repent and change our ways, but if we are innocent and suffer, we should

_____

_____

and _____.

_____

Searching for the good among the bad.

For this exercise you need to see your past through a wide-angle lens that will realistically reveal both the good and the bad of those unwanted, painful events of the past. I am not asking you to call evil "good," nor do I want you to play down the seriousness of evil or excuse the bad that was done. But I do want you to try to connect emotionally with the reality that God will use every situation for good, if we only ask Him.

Corrie ten Boom and her sister demonstrated this when they thanked God for the lice in the concentration camp because this deterred the guards from stopping the prayers and Bible study of the inmates.

You may not be ready for this exercise yet. It may be that the pain is too fresh and you can't see God's hand in the situation. It is OK to be where you are. You don't have to force what you don't feel or understand what is for the moment unfathomable. Just be open and ask God to reveal in His time a new way of looking at your past. If you have a willing heart, one day you will also make the emotional connection and be able to see His plan for the advancement of His kingdom and what this has meant to you and others in your life.

If you are ready to and can think of anything good that God has brought out of a painful event of the past or if you can remember a situation which was a mixture of good and bad, write about it below.

_____

_____

_____

_____

_____

_____

_____

G O D   I S   I N
C O N T R O L

For us to know that God is in control of the bad things that happen to us and still believe that God is good and loving, several things must be true: He knows about the bad; He cares about it; He takes responsibility for it because it exists. He must have a goal or purpose in mind that I can, at least in part, understand.

Does God Know about the Hurt?

I hate the song "From a Distance." I will turn off the radio and listen to silence rather than let my blood pressure rise to the boiling point. The song paints a picture of God sitting on a cloud somewhere looking benignly at the world. He watches an eagle fly and sees everything as blue and green and peaceful as He looks on from His distant perch. The song makes me so angry because it is completely against Scripture. But it also upsets me because if God is just up there wishing me well, I don't need Him. I need Him in my mess. I need Him in my fear. I need Him amid famine and war and pain. I don't need a distant God.

Through the incarnation of Jesus, God got close enough to the world to smell the stench and sweat. He personally experienced pain, rejection, unfair treatment, and questions without answers (Matt. 27:46). Jesus freely acknowledged the fact that both bad and good things happen to all and that these events often have nothing to do with whether or not the person is pleasing to God.

Jesus gave two examples of both good and bad events happening in what seemed like random fashion to individuals totally apart from their moral standing. Look up these two events in Matthew 5:45 and Luke 13:4, and write a few sentences about your reaction to these verses.

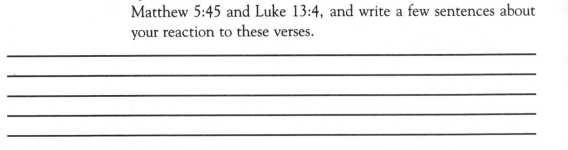

The Bible tells us that God knows the painful things that touch each one of us. In the book of Revelation, Jesus gives John a message for seven churches and tells him that He knows intimately how the people feel, describing their trials and suffering.

I have listed eleven specific things which Jesus said He knew about these individuals. As you read through them, choose one or two which reflect something about your own life, look up the verse, write it out, and carry it with you for one week.

I know how hard you have tried (Rev. 2:2).
I know how patient you have been (Rev. 2:2).
I know how strongly you feel about wicked people and evil (Rev. 2:2).
I know how much you have suffered (Rev. 2:9).
I know about your money problems (Rev. 2:9).
I know the lies others have said about you (Rev. 2:9).
I know where you live and how difficult it is for you there (Rev. 2:13).
I know about the love you have in your heart and your faithfulness (Rev. 2:19).
I know how much strength you have left (Rev. 3:8).
I know the apathy you feel (Rev. 3:15).

Does God Care?
There is only one way to know what someone is feeling: They have to tell us. How do we know if they are telling us the truth?

We cannot know their heart, but we can examine their actions. If someone's words are consistent with their actions, we can believe them; otherwise, we are right to question their words.

What is true of people is even more true of God. The only way we can know what He feels is if He chooses to tell us. Then we can believe Him or not, based on His actions.

God has expressed His feelings through His Word. We know that He feels grief (Eph. 4:30; Ps. 95:10), love (John 3:16), anger (Deut. 9:20), delight (1 Kings 10:9), longing (Jer. 31:20), hate (Rev. 2:15), and many other emotions. He has also told us how He feels when we are in pain.

When Ephraim sinned and wandered away from God, he was punished. But God did not enjoy disciplining Ephraim. In Jeremiah 31:20, God tells us what he felt. "Is Ephraim My dear son? / Is he a pleasant child? / For though I spoke against him, / I earnestly remember him still; / Therefore My heart yearns for him; I will surely have mercy on him."

In Isaiah we read what the Lord felt when His people were hurt. "In all their affliction He was afflicted, / And the Angel of His Presence saved them; / In His love and in His pity He redeemed them; / And He bore them and carried them / All the days of old" (Isa. 63:9). And God seems almost wounded when His love is brought into question. "But Zion said, 'The LORD has forsaken me, / And my Lord has forgotten me.' 'Can a woman forget her nursing child, / And not have compassion on the son of her womb? / Surely they may forget, / Yet I will not forget you'" (Isa. 49:14–15).

These same feelings of compassion are echoed in the New Testament as Jesus saw people troubled and in pain. "When He saw the multitudes, He was moved with compassion for them, because they were weary and scattered, like sheep having no shepherd" (Matt. 9:36).

All of these statements about His feelings would be subject to doubt if God's behavior differed from His words. But fortunately for us, God has taken action to back up what He has said. We can see that action in the following two verses: "Greater love has no one than this, than to lay down one's life for his friends. You are My friends" (John 15:13–14); and "For God so loved the world that He gave His only begotten Son, that whoever believes in Him should not perish but have everlasting life" (John 3:16).

Using your imagination.

For this exercise you do not need a pencil, only your imagination. To perform this exercise you will need a time of quiet relaxation. You might practice it just before you go to sleep tonight or during a moment of quiet devotions in the morning or afternoon. Reading about it now will draw you into the imagery in a small way, but to really give yourself emotionally to the exercise, you will need only think about the scene, preferably with your eyes closed.

Imagine yourself standing at the foot of God's throne. The throne is the centerpiece of all you can see. Everything is related to that massive throne. Before it there stretches a crystalline floor. All around it are people from every country in the world. A little closer in there are twenty-four special dignitaries who fall on their faces and worship the One who is seated high on the throne, lifted up in an unapproachable light. All around the throne itself is a wide rainbow of many colors, with especially beautiful shades of green.

As you look all around you, realizing that you are a small child, you are in awe of the splendor which surrounds you. In the center of the throne is a powerful, soft light, and you can only vaguely see the One who occupies it. You notice a movement in the light, and a hand extends toward you. A deep, thunderous voice calls your name, but you are not afraid. You are invited to approach the light because you are a child of the One who sits there.

Think of yourself walking across the smooth crystalline floor, past the bowed elders, up the steps of the throne and into the light.

Once inside the light you find yourself embraced in strong and loving arms that are as gentle as they are powerful. You rest yourself in the broad lap and every muscle relaxes. You are totally at peace.

Now look back down the path that brought you here. Look out past the light, past the elders, past the multitudes of heaven. You can see dark space and millions of stars. As you continue to look, you center in on one star complex and one star inside that constellation. You look past the other planets, past the moon, past the clouds, and see the earth as a blue and green ball rolling from day to night to day.

As you continue to sit snugly in the lap of God, you are given the ability to stop and start time like a videotape. You decide to roll back to the past, to your town, to your situation that created pain. You see the people as they were at that moment. Then you roll even further back and see the adults in the video when they were children. Now push fast-forward and watch your life move rapidly through the years in one broad sweep.

How does life feel from this perspective? How does it feel to know that this was God's view all along, that He could see and care about all that is on the videotape of your life?

The Bible confirms that God knows intimately the hurts we have faced and He cares. But two questions still remain: Is He willing to take responsibility for the bad experiences? Can I understand why He allowed them to happen? I firmly believe the answer to both questions is yes.

WHO IS RESPONSIBLE FOR THIS MESS?

There is a difference between blame and responsibility. Blame indicates condemnation and guilt. Responsibility only indicates the burden to act rightly because we have the ability to do so.

We Christians are sometimes too quick to try and get the responsibility for the existence of bad things off God's shoulders because we are afraid He will be mad at us for saying He is to blame. We want to take each separate tiny event and put it in a box labeled "blessing" or a box labeled "curse." We will quickly give God credit for the blessing box but not the curse box. We blame the bad stuff on self-will, Satan, demons, or a force of nature.

We had a major plane crash at the Dallas/Fort Worth airport a couple of years ago. Some people were caught and burned in the plane, but many others escaped. As the TV news cameras were interviewing one of the survivors, he spoke of how God had broken the plane in two at the critical moment so that a way of escape was opened. But no one mentioned those who were burned alive. What was God's position concerning them?

We don't talk much about it in Christian circles, but the Bible affirms that God is in control of even bad events. God is not to blame in the sense of condemnation or guilt, but He is responsible for the people who were burned alive and for those who escaped as the plane broke in two.

We are very reluctant to think of God as being responsible for difficult things, but that reluctance is purely our own device. God does not say that about Himself at all.

God is not reluctant to accept responsibility as ruler. When Moses was struggling with God and reluctant to take on the task to which God was sending him, the conversation between the two of them almost reads like God gets ticked. At the last He tells Moses, "Who has made man's mouth? Or who makes the mute, the deaf, the seeing, or the blind? Have not I, the LORD?" (Ex. 4:11). In this passage God clearly lays at His own throne the responsibility for someone being deaf, dumb, or blind.

God never shirks His responsibility. Unlike many in Washington, D.C., where passing the buck is the name of the only game in town, or many of our homes where we strive to prove "it's someone else's fault," God is faithful to His responsibility to rule. And because heaven and earth are totally in His control—when He allows people to do wrong or allows Satan to live or does not stop time—He does not hesitate to take responsibility for those decisions.

Because God claims total power and sovereign control over all things, I have to ask myself some very pointed questions when trouble comes. If pain enters my world because of a tornado, who set the world in motion and created weather in the first place? If Satan sends disease to me, does not God have control over Satan? Did He not form that creature just as He formed me? If my boss chooses to fire me, is not God bigger than my boss? If I do something dumb on my own and cause myself pain by my own free choice, did not God give me that choice?

> I am the LORD, and there is no other;
> There is no God besides Me.
> I will gird you, though you have not known Me,
> That they may know from the rising of the sun
>   to its setting
> That there is none besides Me.
> I am the LORD, and there is no other;
> I form the light and create darkness,
> I make peace and create calamity;
> I, the LORD, do all these things.
>
>   (Isa. 45:5–7)

DOES GOD HAVE A PURPOSE FOR THE BAD?

So far all we have done is to scripturally establish a paradox. We have shown that God knows about our trouble and that He cares. We have also seen that He is all-powerful and willing to take responsibility for letting evil exist. But how can that be? How can He care and take responsibility but then not *do* something!

We said earlier that we are justified in doubting emotions that are spoken if these are contradicted by a person's actions. When it comes to our daily life, we know that we hurt, we hear God say that He cares, and we know that God can change the world to eliminate our hurt if He chooses to do so. We pray. He seemingly does nothing, and we still hurt. How can we trust a God like that? Are we justified in doubting the truth of what He says He feels for us?

The only way we can trust in the middle of this puzzle is if we seriously entertain the possibility that God knows something about this life that we don't.

For myself, that is not too big a step. I can't figure out a simple thing like why my diet won't work. Much less can I understand things that God sets up as everyday events, such as how birds remember migration routes, why no two snowflakes are exactly alike, or how two parents can give birth to a third person who has a separate soul.

Another reason I can accept that things might look a whole lot different from God's viewpoint is that I have had the frustrating experience of trying to explain things to my children when they were two or three that they could not possibly understand. I suspect that the gulf between my mind and God's is even bigger than that between an adult human mind and a two-year-old human mind.

Pure faith should be able to rest at this point. If we just accept the fact that He is God and we are not, we have a degree of comfort if not explanation. Accepting that a good God could let pain exist because He knows more about what is happening than I can understand provides a sense of safety, and if we were really people of faith, that would be enough.

But God has given us a bit more than that. He was not forced to go this extra step, but He did. Perhaps this is part of what Jesus meant when He said, "You are My friends . . . No longer do I call you servants, for a servant does not know what his master is doing; but I have called you friends" (John 15:14–15).

When we begin listening and studying all the many things God has shared with us about His reasons and His goals, we could easily fill another book. We know that just a few of the goals God has in mind are: (1) To again establish an earth and a heaven where the mix-up of good and bad is no longer part of the human experience. He is going to get all the bad in one place (hell) and all the good in another place (heaven) and never will they be mixed up again (See Rev. 19—22; Rev. 22:11); (2) He is also in the process of shaping the character of each Christian into the likeness of Jesus (Rom. 8:28–29); (3) He is eliminating sin's damage in individual lives (1 John 3:8); and (4) He is also providing a Show-and-Tell example to all creation, giving proof of His own character of love and grace (Eph. 2:6–7).

But I would like to look at the purpose of God from a slightly different angle. I want to examine the doors through which pain enters our life and think about reasons God might have for not shutting those doors. For the rest of this chapter we will look at two doors, time and circumstance, and in the next section we will look at the third door, choice.

Time

When viewed from an eternal perspective, time is a new phenomenon. It hasn't always existed, and it will cease to be (Rev. 10:6–7). But for now, it rules our bodies and much of our thinking. We consider it in almost all of our actions, forgetting that it is only a temporary part of our total experience. Time is the source of much of our pain and confusion.

When I spoke in the Chicago area a few months ago, I was invited to Sunday dinner by a delightful family. I have seldom experienced a more open, loving home. Neighbors dropped in and out. They seemed more like extended family than visitors. In the late afternoon we sang around an old upright piano, and a young missionary couple was invited in to join us.

After several hours of getting to know each other, I discovered the deep heartache that this couple had recently suffered. They were home on leave from Bangladesh when the mother went in to check on their firstborn child who was only three months old. He was dead.

Without warning, pain had blasted into the lives of these two young servants of the Lord. There was no explanation for a tragedy like this and no comfort in this world.

As the husband and wife talked a little about their pain and loss, they both spoke of their faith. They believed that Spencer Jonathan Unsel was in heaven and home with the Lord. They both believed they would see him again. But as the tears gently flowed down the mother's cheeks she said, "It is just that it will be so long, and I miss him now!" The thought of time made the separation more painful. Would he be a baby when they saw him again? Would he be grown? How could they possibly manage their pain between now and then? What about the lost years of watching their baby grow? How could God ever replace that?

How many of your own questions about the goodness of God relate to the pain which time brings into your life? We wait for God's answer to prayer. We wait for a fresh wound to heal. We wait for guidance. We wait, hoping situations will change. We wait for Jesus to come again and get us out of this mess. When you consider it, time has probably been very much involved in the painful situations of your life.

Look back to the exercise on page 153 and think about the three questions you wrote to God. How was time involved in the difficult realities that prompted these questions? How could it have been different if you controlled time?

Why does God leave the door of time open? Pain comes through that door. Couldn't a God who created time and will one day stop it just hurry it up a bit when we are hurting?

I consistently prayed a particular prayer for twenty years before God finally said no. Why so long, Lord? What was Your goal? What were You trying to accomplish? What were Your purpose and reason?

Perhaps God does not shut the door of time because pain is not the only thing which enters through this door.

Hope also comes through the door of time.

If there were no time, we could never experience hope. As Paul says, "But hope that is seen is not hope; for why does one still hope for what he sees? But if we hope for what we do not see, then we eagerly wait for it with perseverance" (Rom.

8:24–25). Hope enables us to endure the pain of this world. Hope provides a refuge. We, like David, can rest in the hope of knowing that God will never leave us (Acts 2:26–27).

Circumstance

Another door through which pain enters our life is the door of circumstance. I could have called it "chance," but that would imply accident and lack of control, and we have already established that those things don't really exist because God is in control of all things.

By "circumstance" I mean those unexplainable, illogical tragedies that appear to come from being in the wrong place at the wrong time. A flood destroys twenty-five houses, and ours is one of them. We resign our job and move our family 1500 miles to take advantage of what looks like a golden opportunity, and six months later the company folds. We practice healthy living and never smoke or drink, but we end up with lung cancer anyway.

Could God shut the door of circumstance? Could He create a world where bad things only happen to bad people? Of course He could, but He doesn't. Christ said, "[God] . . . sends rain on the just and on the unjust" (Matt. 5:45). Painful circumstances cause us to seek God and His wisdom.

Think back over your questions in the exercise on page 153. How many of them involve the sufferings of innocent people?

Why does God leave the door of circumstance open? The pain of unexplainable tragedy forces us to ask God for an explanation. We seek His wisdom, and we have faith that He will reveal it to us. You see, faith, as well as pain, enters through the door of circumstance.

Faith is what draws us closer to God. Our faith can heal the wounds of painful circumstances. The Bible tells us of the woman who was healed when she touched the hem of Jesus' garment. Do you remember what He said to her? "Be of good cheer, daughter; your *faith* has made you well" (Matt. 9:22, italics mine).

The pain that comes through the door is temporary, but the faith that also enters in allows our soul to have everlasting peace (Luke 7:50).

SUMMATION

Our environment has helped to shape and mold us. It is a vital part of our identity. When that environment became painful, we may have tried to run—away from the pain, away from ourselves—leaving a part of self behind.

With hope and faith we can learn to accept the past. We can ask God to go with us on our journey. With His love and guidance we will find those parts of ourselves we once thought were lost forever. For He remembers everything; He knows us intimately and will give us peace and understanding. All we have to do is ask.

What knowledge of yourself has God revealed to you so far? As you complete the summation page, remember what Jesus taught in Matthew 7:7–8:

"Ask, and it will be given to you; seek, and you will find; knock, and it will be opened to you. For everyone who asks receives, and he who seeks finds, and to him who knocks it will be opened."

Personal Summation:

PART FOUR

Choice,
Self Changed
Through Will
and Decision

CHAPTER 10 ❧

Non-moral Choice: A Gift of Self-freedom

I was driving slowly down the quiet, tree-lined street that leads to my apartment when a teenage boy pulled along beside me waving frantically and motioning for me to roll down my window. Because I live only two blocks from the high school and teenage drivers are common in our area, I was not concerned about rolling down my window. When I did, he shouted, "Pro-Choice!" and sped away, evidently responding to the pro-life bumper sticker on my car.

If there is one word that could possibly characterize America in the '90s it might be the word *choice*. Not just choice about abortion but choice about everything. Individual rights have taken center stage above all else.

"My right to be me" has become the theme song of an entire generation. "Do your own thing" no matter if society approves or not, no matter who it hurts.

At the other end of the scale are the domineering and authoritarian individuals who deny others the right to choose anything. These are the mothers, husbands, neighbors, and bosses who suck the life and spontaneity out of everyone around them, viewing any desire for individual choice as an act of rebellion.

Recently a parent called me to make an appointment for a twelve-year-old daughter who was "rebellious." After listening to a description of the problem, I suggested they make a family appointment.

As the family of five took their seats, the twelve-year-old, who was the oldest child, sat a little apart from the rest. While she was not disruptive, neither was she attentive. She busied herself counting the ceiling tiles, playing with her fingers, and swinging her chair around until she had her back to the group.

The mother and father spent about a half-hour talking about her attitude, a hat that she insisted on wearing indoors, and her refusal to take a bath in the morning rather than the evening, but they provided little concrete evidence of what is classically thought of as rebellion. When I pressed for a specific example, the mother thought a moment and then volunteered the following story.

The entire family had gone to the mall last week. School was beginning and the children needed clothes. The classmates of the oldest girl most often wore jeans and knit T-shirts to class, and the parents had no objection to that style of dress.

Their daughter chose a black shirt from the rack. It did not have offensive pictures or phrases on it. It was just a plain black shirt.

But the mother knew about fashion and how things should be. Her daughter did not look good in black. She needed pastels. No black was to be permitted. The mother held up a light blue shirt and a pink one and insisted that one of these must be chosen and no other. A verbal argument followed and the girl vowed that if she could not have the black one, she would not wear anything else. If her mother bought the blue one, it could hang in the closet, unworn, forever.

I knew it was a risky step to take, but I picked up a Bible from the desk and held it up as I reminded the group, "Never in all the Holy Word of God does it ever say, 'Thou shalt not wear black T-shirts.'" For the first time, the twelve-year-old swung her chair around and began to pay attention.

The Word does say that children are to obey their parents (Eph. 6:1), but it also says that parents should not frustrate their children to the point of anger (Eph. 6:4). Children and adults need to be able to express themselves without unnecessary restrictions.

No doubt there was a good deal of fight in this feisty preteen, but it was the fight of a drowning person gasping for air. She did not want to rebel against her parents or their moral standards, she just wanted room to breathe and be herself.

Both the teen from the pro-choice viewpoint and the girl with the black T-shirt were concerned with freedom of choice. God is concerned with that freedom too. He has given us this freedom for expression and joy; He has made rules to govern choice and set limitations on it; and He has also chosen to let us choose to have a Father-child relationship with Him.

Choice is important. Choice helps define who we are.

CHOICE: A FACTOR THAT MOLDS US

Our genetics come to us prepackaged and our environment surrounds us without our permission. But if this were all that made us unique, people would be like snowflakes: Each different but each cold and changed only by the world into which each falls. Choice makes us an active participant in changing what has been into what can be.

Choice is as much a gift of God as our heritage and our heartbeat. Whether we want it or we don't, choice and the responsibility it involves have been dropped in our lap, and we cannot deny it. Even if we decide not to decide, we are still making a choice. If we are faced with two possibilities and decide that we will not choose either one, that decision in itself becomes a choice, and it has consequences just like any other choice.

Having the freedom to choose is one of the ways that we are created in God's image. The Bible frequently talks about God's choices. It even says that He has chosen us (John 15:16).

Genetics and environment have molded us, and so have the

choices we have made. Sometimes we have looked carefully at our options and chosen what we thought was best for the long term. Other times we have jumped first and thought later, scarcely even realizing that what we were doing was making a choice. But both kinds of choices, whether thought out or not, expressed our present and shaped our future.

There are basically two kinds of choices: non-moral and moral. God allows both and He gives freedom and responsibility with each. The teen that was shouting "Pro-Choice!" was making a moral choice. The teen who wanted a black T-shirt was concerned with a non-moral choice of self-expression.

One of the things you have altered by choice is your body. For example, fingernails don't genetically come in fire-engine red. If you paint yours, you are expressing individuality and identity. By choice you are responding to the natural color you were given and altering it to something you like better. The same is true for the cut and style of your hair, exercise that has reshaped your body, dieting, face-lifts, girdles, padded bras, high heels, wigs, and makeup. Write a paragraph examining how you have chosen to accent, change, or hide part of what was given to you genetically.

_____

_____

_____

_____

_____

_____

NON-MORAL CHOICES

We have just discussed examples of non-moral choices. These free, non-moral choices are a delightful adventure in self-expression, and they involve our body, our friends, what we read, how we choose to express our emotions, and the kind of food we like to eat.

In a well-functioning family, the training of children in non-moral choices begins early and ends around the mid-teens. A two-year-old has to have most of his choices about clothing, personal resources, and self-expression made for him by his parents. A seven-year-old has more choice in these matters. And a fifteen-year-old should have free reign over most of his non-moral choices (remember, I said *most*).

However, families sometimes err to one extreme on the spectrum of choice. Either they provide no structure and guidance, or they try to make every choice for the child from how to spend an allowance to hairstyle. Either of these extremes prevents the child from learning the joy of self-expression.

A child cannot learn who she is if she is never allowed to express individuality and identity, neither can she be comfortable with who she is if a lack of guidance leaves her unsure and embarrassed or if continual criticism makes her doubt every expression of self.

Think back to your early teen years. How much freedom were you given in each of the following areas? Mark the degree of freedom by circling a number on the scale. Do the exercise a second time and mark the degree of criticism you received for your choices by boxing in the appropriate number.

Choice of clothing

   1   2   3   4   5   6   7   8   9   10

Choice of friends

   1   2   3   4   5   6   7   8   9   10

Choice of how you used time

   1   2   3   4   5   6   7   8   9   10

Choice of how you used personal money

   1   2   3   4   5   6   7   8   9   10

Choice of church activities

   1   2   3   4   5   6   7   8   9   10

Choice of decor in your room

    1   2   3   4   5   6   7   8   9   10

Choice of hairstyle

    1   2   3   4   5   6   7   8   9   10

Choice of extracurricular school activities

    1   2   3   4   5   6   7   8   9   10

Choice of participation in family outings

    1   2   3   4   5   6   7   8   9   10

This scale has no right or wrong answers. It should help give you an idea of the family structure at the time you were being trained about choice.

There are hundreds, perhaps thousands, of ways that you express your identity through non-moral choices, but I have limited this exercise to fifteen.

If I were answering for myself I would include such statements as: I am a person who chooses red cars; I am a person who chooses to work in business suits; I am a person who chooses to dress very casual when not in a business suit; I am a person who chooses Mexican food over fish.

How have you chosen to express yourself? Complete the following statements with the first things that come to your mind. You may add to the list using separate sheets of paper if you like.

1. I am a person who chooses

_____

_____

2. I am a person who chooses

_____

_____

3. I am a person who chooses

_____

_____

4. I am a person who chooses

_____

_____

5. I am a person who chooses

_____

_____

6. I am a person who chooses

_____

_____

7. I am a person who chooses

_____

_____

8. I am a person who chooses

_____

_____

9. I am a person who chooses

_____

_____

10. I am a person who chooses

_____

_____

11. I am a person who chooses

_____

_____

12. I am a person who chooses

_____

_____

13. I am a person who chooses

_____

_____

14. I am a person who chooses

_____

_____

15. I am a person who chooses

_____

_____

NON-MORAL SPIRITUAL CHOICES

There are many kinds of non-moral choices. The field is as broad as the variety of human experience is wide. There are even non-moral spiritual choices.

Paul talked of one group of Christians who celebrated particular holidays to honor the Lord and of another set of Christians who chose to honor the Lord by treating every day alike. Neither was right nor wrong. Both choices were good (Rom. 14:6).

There are probably some forms of spiritual expression that you like better than others, and there may be some forms that you would be very uncomfortable with. You may choose a congregation where everyone prays out loud at the same time, or you may choose a corporate service where every motion is written in the bulletin a week in advance and the choir is rehearsed to a professional tone. You may be blessed by kneeling to pray, or the best times you have with the Lord may be while jogging with a

Walkman, playing praise tapes. These are all non-moral spiritual choices.

What non-moral choices have you made concerning your spiritual expression of faith? In the spaces below, try to list them, beginning with those that please you most.

1. _____
2. _____
3. _____
4. _____
5. _____

What choices are you currently making concerning your worship both privately and corporately?

_____
_____
_____

THE SINS OF NON-MORAL CHOICE

While non-moral choice is a sinless process, there can be secret sins wrapped inside. It can be like a lovely cake with a rotten fish baked in its core.

It is not a sin to choose to own a fur coat unless it feeds the pride of the wearer or robs people of money the Lord meant to go for their care or is used to make those without such a luxury feel inferior. In this case, a non-moral choice has a rotten fish at its heart.

It seems that there are at least three ways sin most often creeps into non-moral choice: (1) when we make others responsible for our choices; (2) when we use our choices to hide; or (3) when we refuse to let others have choices of their own.

Making Others Responsible for Our Choices

One of the most common sins involving choice is to avoid God's gift because we are afraid of others. We choose what we think others want us to choose then gripe because they "forced" us into what we did not want.

I remember one woman complaining that her husband "made" her give up a relationship with a girlfriend. When she and her husband first married, she saw the friend several times a week, spent hours on the phone, and went somewhere with her at least one night a week. When her husband protested, she dropped the entire relationship with great bitterness. When I asked why she didn't see the friend once a week during the day and limit her calls, she sighed like a martyr. It was no use. He would have been angry at her. "So, what?" I asked. "He wasn't telling you that you could never see your friend, and you won't die if he gets angry." She was appalled at the suggestion. She preferred to assume the role of a martyr rather than risk the unpleasant feeling of knowing that her husband was not altogether pleased. It was easier to blame him than to take responsibility for her choice.

I have seen this same scenario repeatedly. There was the husband who moaned because his wife "made" him give her his entire paycheck to manage along with her paycheck and he could never go to lunch or buy a newspaper without asking her for money. And the woman whose children "made" her take them so many places she could never get her own work done; and the friend who was "forced" to talk on the phone for hours with others who needed counsel and a shoulder to cry on, wearing her down and making her depressed all the time.

Each of these people had the same problem. They avoided their responsibility in governing their life, choices, and time because they could not stand the thought that someone else might be mad or not approve of their choice.

If some choices are voluntarily given away because of our desire to please others, that is grace. But if we refuse to take charge of our lives and hold others responsible for choices that damage or distress us, we are refusing to grow up.

Most of us have probably experienced this dynamic in one way or another. Have you ever asked someone where they would like to eat and hear them say, "Oh, it doesn't matter"? Then after making several trips on that merry-go-round, you finally choose, and they get mad because you made the wrong choice? This humorous example isn't funny if you must stay in close relation with someone who is constantly forcing the choice onto you, and then blowing up when you don't choose to please them.

Have you felt manipulated by others who refuse to take responsibility for their choices? Has the Lord convicted you that this is a problem in your relationships with others? Do you blame them because you didn't want to take the responsibility for personal choice? Write a few lines about it below.

_____

_____

_____

_____

_____

_____

Using Our Choices to Hide

One of the purposes of non-moral choice is to express to the outside world who we are on the inside, but because the world can see only the outward expression and not the inner person, changing and rearranging our outward expression can be used to hide what is really inside.

For example, strong makeup and unusual clothes could be an expression of a woman who is naturally sanguine and a bit flamboyant, someone who enjoys being and looking a little different from most of her peers. If done within the bounds of social norm and propriety, this is not a sin. But if the clothes and makeup are used to hide a soul that is frightened or if they are an overreaction for someone who is ashamed of their natural desire to withdraw, these things can become a lie.

If you ever ask yourself, "Why do I keep doing this when I don't even like it?" you may be hiding behind a choice. Perhaps you worry about impressing others and deny your claim to the freedom God gave you to be yourself. If you have used choices to hide or if you know of someone else who does, write a few lines about it below.

_____

_____

_____

_____

_____

_____

Denying Others Their Own Choices

Using personal choices in a sinful way, such as refusing to take responsibility or hiding, is fairly common, but perhaps the most common sin of all is not the management of our own choice but our effort to manage the choices of others.

It's easy to see this sin in the lives of others. I seldom find someone who has not had a friend, a husband, a boss, or a parent who tried to control, advise, or manipulate them in some way. But, strangely, we can almost never see this sin in ourselves.

Most often those who try to control others do so because they want to "help" and because they believe they know the "right" or "best" way. They are like the mother at the beginning of our story who knew her daughter did not look her best in black; she was determined to have the "best" for her daughter even if it destroyed the relationship, made everyone miserable, and turned her daughter into a rebel. It was more important to the mother that each decision be "right" than that her daughter become a living soul with a mind and heart of her own.

Some sins travel in pairs: Like adultery and lying, or bitterness and revenge. The sin of controlling the choices of others is like that too. People who deny others their free choice often fail to take responsibility for their own choices. The Bible calls these people sinners, but pop-psychologists call them codependents.

Have you ever felt controlled by someone who refused to let you live your own life? Has the Lord convicted you that this is an area you need to work on? Write a few lines about it below.

_____

_____

_____

_____

_____

_____

MORAL CHOICE

There is only one criteria for judging whether a choice is moral or non-moral—the Bible. Nothing else works; not our conscience, our reasoning, our judgment, not our likes and dislikes. If the Bible says it is wrong, then it *is* wrong. If the Bible says it is right, then it *is* right. Where the Bible is silent, we must make a non-moral choice which is up to the individual and not subject to outside interference.

Each moral choice we make has consequences. We read about them in Galatians 6:7–8: "Do not be deceived, God is not mocked; for whatever a man sows, that he will also reap. For he who sows to his flesh will of the flesh reap corruption, but he who sows to the Spirit will of the Spirit reap everlasting life."

You have likely made some good moral choices in your life. These can be as mild as choosing to discipline yourself by breaking the habit of fingernail biting (any habit that has control of us is a sin) or as major as deciding not to marry someone because he is not a Christian and you want to be obedient to the Word (2 Cor. 6:14).

To help you think about some of the good moral choices you have made, try to connect each of the following sentences with a specific incident from your life. Place a check by any of the things that apply to you.

1. ☐ I chose to let go of an offense someone committed against me.

2. ☐ I chose to tell the truth even though it was hard.

3. ☐ I chose to yield to reality rather than fight what I could not change.

4. ☐ I chose not to steal.

5. ☐ I chose to remain sexually pure.

6. ☐ I chose to give credit to others when they earned it.

7. ☐ I chose to forgive.

8. ☐ I chose not to have an affair even though I was tempted.

9. ☐ I chose to control my temper.

10. ☐ I chose to pay my debts.

11. ☐ I chose to be unselfish.

12. ☐ I chose to make God a priority in my life.

13. ☐ I chose to keep a confidence.

14. ☐ I chose to keep a promise.

15. ☐ I chose to give money and/or goods to someone in need.

There are probably other correct moral choices that you have made. Continue this exercise by writing about some of them as you complete the sentences below. Some ideas might include: Have you disciplined yourself by breaking a habit? Have you chosen to continue in church? Do you seek to know God better? Have you decided to stick with a difficult marriage? Did you choose to complete college despite obstacles? Have you chosen to learn to love someone?

16. ☐ I chose _____
_____.

17. ☐ I chose _____
_____.

18. ☐ I chose _____
_____.

19. ☐ I chose _____
_____.

20. ☐ I chose _____
_____.

WRONG MORAL CHOICE

When we look at wrong moral choices, we are looking at sin. The apostle Paul referred to the working of sin as a "mystery" (2 Thess. 2:7). The whole idea of sin—why it is on earth, why we can't get rid of it, and how we can break free from the damage it has done to us—is a mystery that we may never fully understand while we are on earth. But if we will turn to God, we can accept this fact and live our lives in peace as we learn more about God's plan for us.

Living in peace is not easy when we have made a wrong moral choice. Words like *shame, guilt, trapped, self-hate,* and *punishment* crawl around like so many worms inside our soul, leaving us anything but peaceful. We need a way out of the mess. But at times, God's method of escape can seem more painful than simply learning to live with the worms!

Our first step toward peace is to face what we have done, without excusing or rationalizing. We look at our wrong moral choice and call it what God calls it—sin.

We may find it difficult to acknowledge our wrong moral choices for what they were—choices. We don't want to use that word. Our first instinct is to think about the circumstance, and the pressure from other people, and our youth at the time, and how quickly things happened, and a dozen and one other exceptions and reasons that help us avoid saying, "I chose to do wrong."

Listed below are a few of the more common choices that leave us with a few worms like guilt and shame. Mark those that apply to you, letting yourself fully take the impact of the idea of choice without excuses.

1. ☐ I chose to take revenge and get even.

2. ☐ I chose to tell a lie.

3. ☐ I chose to be rebellious in spirit.

4. ☐ I chose to steal.

5. ☐ I chose to have an abortion.

6. ☐ I chose to cheat.

7. ☐ I chose to become bitter and resisted forgiving.

8. ☐ I chose to have an affair.

9. ☐ I chose to be cruel to an animal.

10. ☐ I chose not to pay back the money I owed.

11. ☐ I chose to be selfish.

12. ☐ I chose to put God last in my life.

13. ☐ I chose to gossip and tear down another's reputation.

14. ☐ I chose to push my responsibility off on another.

15. ☐ I chose to engage in premarital sex.

Are there other choices that you regret? Did you give away your virginity and then regret it? Is there a lie still haunting you? Did you make a hasty decision to divorce? Did you choose to become involved with alcohol or drugs? Can you even bear to put on paper those things that are the most secret, painful sins of choice? Continue this exercise by finishing the sentences below, filling in those things that haunt you.

16. ☐ I chose _____

_____.

17. ☐ I chose _____

_____.

18. ☐ I chose _____

_____.

19. ☐ I chose _____

_____.

20. ☐ I chose _____

_____.

THE WORMS
CHOICE LEAVES
BEHIND

We are never really lost; we simply feel lost because we have rejected so many pieces of ourselves. Our goal is to find those rejected parts and accept them once again as pieces of who we are. But how can that be done when wrong moral choices and unhappy situations are sprinkled all along the path? How can we possibly accept as our own these things that are rotten and full of worms? These bad choices are often things that God doesn't like any more than we do. How can we embrace them?

If we are going to learn to accept our history of choice, we will have to learn how to deal with the worms that are left behind when wrong choices are made. These worms come in two varieties. There are the black worms of guilt when we have made a wrong choice and the red worms of bitterness when someone else has made a wrong choice and violated us. We must learn how to cleanse our memories of the worms that devour and repulse us before we can possibly embrace them.

There is only one cleansing agent for worms: forgiveness. We must learn to forgive others and to forgive ourselves. The next two chapters are devoted to helping us do that. Chapter 11 addresses guilt, and Chapter 12 will complete this section with a discussion of how to forgive others and ourselves.

But before you go on, complete this chapter by filling in the personal summation page. You may want to write questions you have concerning guilt and forgiveness, or write a paragraph about what you have emotionally experienced as you worked through this chapter on choice.

Personal Summation:

CHAPTER 11

Moral Choice: The Stain and the Pain

A wrong choice can hatch an egg of guilt that if not cleansed immediately grows into a worm that eats at our very vitals. If this creature gets strong enough, it can drive a wedge between us and God, making us afraid to approach the only Solution and cutting us off from any peace we might have known.

We all know the anguish that can be caused by guilt—the churning in the stomach, the desire to run and hide, the flushed cheeks, and defensive stance. Guilt can also affect our body.

David noted the physical manifestations in his own body, saying, "My bones grew old / Through my groaning all the day long. / For day and night Your hand was heavy upon me; / My vitality was turned into the drought of summer" (Ps. 32:3–4).

Unrelenting feelings of guilt can cause ulcers, high blood pressure, panic attacks, headaches, sweating, dry mouth, tense muscles, heart palpitations, and the most common symptom of all—depression. It has been said that if we could teach people to forgive themselves and let go of guilt, we could empty most of our mental institutions and take one-third of the people off medication. From what I have seen, I find that easy to believe.

You may have experienced feelings of guilt as you worked through the last chapter. With those feelings fresh on your heart, look over the list below. Which words and phrases describe your feelings of guilt? Circle those words.

dirty	exposed	to blame	rejected
derelict	worthless	reprehensible	hot
caught	trapped	naked	abandoned
alone	helpless	angry	defensive
agitated	frightened	without hope	

There is another worm that comes from choice. Someone else makes a wrong choice that hurts us, and if that wound is not healed, the worm of bitterness grows.

Perhaps someone cheated us, abandoned us, abused us, or disappointed us. If I leave work one night and get mugged in the parking lot, someone else has hurt me through a wrong choice they made. If I allow myself to become bitter over my experiences, I not only hurt myself—I also deny God's Spirit the opportunity to heal me so that I can be an example of His grace.

Bitterness is more than the natural response of anger at being hurt. It is anger that has sat around and has been fed and nurtured rather than resolved. Anger is not a sin (Eph. 4:26), but bitterness is (v. 31).

Unless you are very unusual, you probably know how it feels to be bitter. As you try to recall your feelings of bitterness, look at the list of words and phrases below. Circle those that describe what you have experienced.

fury	revenge	hate	desire to hurt
grief	ripped off	violated	spiteful
fire in my bones	rage	insulted	violent
cheated	malicious	malignant	vicious
controlled by anger			

Between the list of words for guilt and those for bitterness, we have a cornucopia of human suffering. Pain is written into every line.

In the last section we looked at two ways pain enters our life: time and circumstance. But even more pain enters our life through choice. Some have estimated that 85 percent of the pain we endure is self-inflicted; we can trace it back to the poor choices we have made. When we add to that the pain caused by choices that others have made, we understand how great a factor choice is in the creation of pain.

Because so much pain comes through the door of choice, we may ask ourselves why God continues to allow bad choices. Let's explore the value of the freedom of choice. We will do this by examining the wrong choices made by others.

WHEN OTHERS MAKE A WRONG CHOICE

Why does God choose to leave the door of choice open for human involvement? He could close it, you know. He is sovereign, and at any time He could stop others from making wrong choices against us, and He could make it impossible for us to make a wrong choice.

What does He hope to gain by leaving the door open and letting pain rush into our lives? We saw that hope as well as pain came through the door of time, and both faith and pain came through the door of circumstance. But what travels with pain through the door of choice?

Let's go back for a moment to the story of Chelsey, the little girl who prayed that Jesus would keep Grandpa away and not let her be abused again. What would you have done if you had been God Almighty sitting on the throne of the universe that night?

I know what I would have done. I would have sent a lightning bolt to fry Grandpa if he even thought about stepping toward that door. I would never let him use his free choice in such a vile way. If not a lightning bolt, then at least a heart attack would have been appropriate at that moment.

But if I were to play God-for-a-night, I would consider others besides that one child. What about the little boy on the other side of town who is being physically abused by his mom? Do I take away the choice of that abuser and force her to do right? What about the hundreds of children starving in refugee camps because of civil wars? Will I ignore them just because they have never heard the name of Jesus and don't know how to pray? I could stop those wars by just rearranging the minds of the soldiers and political leaders. I could force them to think nice thoughts and make them cooperate with each other.

What about the other wrong moral choices in the world? If I am God, where will I draw the line? Will I take away the choice of the drug addict who says he is hurting no one but himself? Will I take away the choice of the preacher who is teaching false doctrine and leading people into hell? Will I take away the choice of the frustrated, tired mother who yells at her four-year-old and then later feels guilty? If I were God, I could fix her so she would never make that mistake.

Well, if I am God, I guess I will just have to take away everyone's ability to make any wrong choice of any kind. Wouldn't that create a peaceful world?

What would our world be like if we lost our ability to choose? Yes, it would probably be peaceful. But what kind of people would we be? We would be robots, not people created in the image of God. And if we lost our ability to choose, we would also lose our ability to love because there is no love without choice. We would be living in a world without love.

In my younger days, I gave birth to three children in four years. These three were in addition to the oldest child who had a five-year head start on them. The day I brought home number four, number two came down with a 104 degree fever. The next few years were interesting to say the least.

I remember being so tired one night that as I rocked one of my babies and he cried, I cried too. I was at the point of exhaustion. Why didn't I just walk off and leave the baby and get some sleep? The answer is simple. Despite my tears and weariness I chose to stay because I loved my son. Had I been forced to stay, I would have been behaving according to the rules of love, but I really would have been a robot performing a task. Because I could choose to stay, I was a mother showing love to her child.

Our prime example of love is Jesus. No love is greater than His love. The ultimate act of love was Calvary, and we know that this act was a voluntary choice. Jesus could have walked off the job at any time (Matt. 26:52–54), but He chose to stay because He could see a future in our salvation and He judged love to be worth it (Heb. 12:2).

Think for a moment. Would we call Calvary an act of love if Jesus had no choice? Would we say that God loved us if Jesus had been forced to provide salvation for us? God's ultimate freedom is what allows God's ultimate love.

Faith comes to us because of unexplainable circumstances in our lives. Hope comes because of time. Love comes to us because we have free choice.

Use the space below to illustrate this idea. You might decide to draw the three doors or write in calligraphy or draw symbols showing how one gives birth to the other or how all travel with pain as they come to us. Use your imagination.

WHAT IF YOU WERE GOD?

I occasionally run abuse recovery groups. We talk about people who have used their free will to hurt, and I ask them, "What would you choose if you were God? Would you choose a world of robots without choice, everything decided for you with no mysteries and no time, or would you choose the world which God has created, knowing that He will use all these things for our growth and to make us more like Him?"

Most often people answer that they would choose the world as it is now, trusting that God will manage the temporary pain of life. But sometimes someone will answer no, preferring a world of robots to a world where pain is possible.

What about you? Which world would you choose? Of course, it is only an academic question because this is God's world, not ours, but we may learn something about ourselves by honestly considering the question.

Write out your answers to the questions previously discussed. Which world would you choose?

_____

_____

_____

_____

_____

If you chose a world of freedom, time, and mystery, can you trust God with the pain that also comes with that choice? If you chose a world of robots, no mysteries, and without time, can you trust a God whose choice is different from what you think is best and allow Him to put these things in your life even though you would have chosen a different world?

Our freedom to choose brings the experience of love into our lives when we use that freedom the way God intended. But remember the pain and the worms? They also come through the door of choice. The agony of guilt aimed at myself and the agony of bitterness aimed at others rush through the door when wrong choices are made.

In the next chapter we will explore the problems of wrong choices made by others and the bitterness that can result. But for the rest of this chapter, we will look at the guilt we experience when we are the one making the wrong choice, or, perhaps more accurately, when we are the one making what we *think* is a wrong choice.

Everyone is born with an internal compass pointing out the directions of right and wrong. We call that compass a conscience, and it is a natural part of God's creation. But, like every other gift of God, it can go a little haywire in this cursed world.

THE WARPED COMPASS

I suppose my naivete could have been explained by my youth. After all, I was a new bride of seventeen, and it was the first time I had ventured outside my tiny, rural hometown. But it appalled and amazed me as I watched my friend Frank pull the ribbons and miscellaneous Christmas decorations from his pockets. I could not believe that he could be so calm and unconcerned about what to me was a major sin.

Frank and his new wife and Bill and myself had only recently become acquainted as we all joined in assignment at our new military base. We had gone shopping for the fast-approaching holidays, and while in the store Frank had helped himself to many small items. As we left the store and continued down the street, Frank began to pull all the trinkets from his pockets and bragged about how smart he was for stealing them. I couldn't believe my eyes! I had never seen anyone steal before. And when they started talking about sniffing glue and drinking alcohol, I nearly dropped my teeth in surprise. I didn't know nice people ever did things like that.

But the most astonishing thing of all was that Frank was surprised at my surprise. We looked at one other as though each had come from separate planets. I could not understand how he could brag about stealing without embarrassment or shame, and he could not understand why someone would be ashamed of shoplifting.

My own conscience hounded me continually with deep pangs of guilt for the smallest infractions of self-made rules, while Frank's conscience was totally silent even when he told of how he once robbed a train!

I don't think that Frank ever had to worry about cleaning out the guilt from his soul, but for me it was a major project that never seemed to be completed. In a way, I almost envied him. My conscience beat and hounded me. I felt as though I should continually apologize for my very existence.

How tender is your conscience compared to those around you? Do you find yourself apologizing for everything? Do you find your heart as cold as a rock? Do you take on the guilt of others while excusing their behavior? Below you will find a scale from zero to ten. Assuming zero is no conscience and ten is someone who feels guilty all the time for everything and everyone, and five is a perfect balance of how God would desire to have guilt work in our life, grade yourself by circling a number on the scale.

0   1   2   3   4   5   6   7   8   9   10

WHERE DO FEELINGS OF GUILT COME FROM?

Why was there such a difference between Frank's conscience and mine? How could he be so wrong according to God's Word and not feel a thing, while I tried with all my heart and soul to be clean yet felt guilty all the time? The truth is that the conscience we inherited from Adam is kind of dumb. Feelings of guilt can come from many sources, and they often have little connection with the reality of guilt.

Every capacity that God gave us is good when used in the manner for which it was intended. The capacity for sex, the capacity for anger, the capacity for fear, and the capacity for guilt are all good when they serve the proper purpose. The correct function for the capacity of guilt is to drive us to God, but our compass of conscience gets messed up easily. It feels the feelings of guilt, but can make no judgment on the validity of those feelings.

Guilt feelings come from three sources: Satan, social training, and the Holy Spirit. All three feel exactly the same, but each requires a different response from us before the feelings can be resolved.

Satan

We are first introduced to Satan's accusatory powers in the book of Job where we see him standing before God accusing Job of insincerity (Job 1:6–12). In the book of Revelation, we are told that he is continually accusing all Christians before the throne of God (Rev. 12:10). And evidently those accusations are not for God's ears only, for it is said that he has the ability to throw fiery darts at our own minds (Eph. 6:16), and I know of no fiery darts worse than accusations of guilt.

Because Satan is a liar and has always been the father of lies (John 8:44), it does not matter to him if he throws a dart of guilty feelings based on a lie or a dart based on the truth. Either way he has created pain and confusion in our life, and that is the goal. When we are feeling the weight of guilt, we need to check it out. Are we really guilty of some unconfessed sin, or are we feeling guilty because we are being attacked by the father of all lies?

Holy Spirit

The Holy Spirit also gives us feelings of guilt as a gift. His purpose is never to lead us to hate the self that God created but to hate our sin and to recognize our inadequacies.

Jesus told us before He left that one of the jobs of the Holy Spirit would be to convict the entire world and to show them the difference between what is sinful and what is holy, between righteousness and unrighteousness, and between justice and injustice (John 16:8). We also know that we can grieve Him when we do wrong (Eph. 4:30); and because He lives within us, we can feel that grieving in our conscience.

When we are feeling guilty because the devil has accused us, we need to stand in faith against it and refuse to let the feeling rule. But when we feel guilt from the ministry of the Holy Spirit, we must listen and respond immediately.

Sometimes Christians feel guilt and wonder how they can tell if these feelings are Satan attacking them or the Holy Spirit leading them. But the problem is really not as complicated as it may seem at first. There are three simple considerations that will almost always give a quick and accurate answer.

First, Satan drives his slaves, but Jesus leads His sheep. If we are being driven, the feelings may well be coming from the evil one.

Second, the Holy Spirit will always be leading us to hate our sin, but Satan will always be leading us to hate ourselves. If we are beating ourselves over and over for some sin after we have confessed and forsaken it, we are most likely struggling with the evil one. In a case like this, it is not a time to repent but a time to stand in faith and insist that we will believe the Word of God (1 John 1:9), not our feelings.

The third consideration is similar to the second. The Holy Spirit will always have a specific sin in mind. If we feel guilty and cannot identify the specific sin involved, we should pray. If we still cannot identify the sin even though we have honestly searched, our feelings of condemnation are likely coming from the enemy.

When we forsake our sin, the guilt provided by the Holy Spirit stops. If feelings of guilt continue, they are not coming from Him but from a different source.

Social Training

Both Satan and the Holy Spirit can provoke feelings of guilt, but perhaps the most common source of those feelings will be our social training. The Bible talks about our conscience being trained. The author of Hebrews mentions those individuals "who by reason of use have their senses exercised to discern both good and evil" (Heb. 5:14), and Paul talked of those who have a weak conscience due to their past training (1 Cor. 8:7).

Frank's conscience was trained by the street gangs of New York, so he felt absolutely no guilt when he shoplifted small items. My conscience was trained in a hell-fire Baptist church, and I could not say a swear word without carrying a large load of guilt.

How was your conscience trained? Your genetics may have given you a naturally tender heart or a naturally tough one. Your evironment then took over the job as church, school, parents, peers, and others told you what was right and wrong. Your choice was also involved as you accepted guilt or fought against those feelings. If you repeatedly refused to listen to your conscience as it was being trained, you may see a time when you no longer feel the pains of guilt (1 Tim. 4:2).

Listed below are twelve situations which can create feelings of guilt. Some of these involve moral issues but not all. How quickly and how strongly would your conscience respond to each of these situations?

1. You are driving down the street and pass someone with a sign that says "Will work for food."

2. You call in and tell the boss you are sick, but in truth you are simply very tired and want a day off.

3. You tithe exactly 9 percent to the church.

4. Your husband gets angry with you because you failed to pick up an item in town.

5. You say no when asked to serve on a church committee.

6. Your child wants an expensive pair of track shoes, but you can't afford them.

7. You gained five pounds.

8. You enjoyed flirting with your husband's best friend.

9. You felt angry and it showed.

10. You cheated on your income tax.

11. Your clothes are obviously more expensive than those of most others in your church.

12. Your boss points out a mistake you made.

Each individual conscience will respond in a slightly different way to this list. One will feel nothing when cheating on their income tax or lying to a boss; however, these moral issues involve true guilt. Another will respond with strong feelings of guilt over gaining five pounds or a husband's anger.

When we have feelings of guilt over social training that is not in line with the Word of God, we must insist that our soul not pay any attention to those feelings, but draw guidance only from the Bible. The guilty feelings may still be there for a while, but if we continue to ignore them and walk in the freedom of His Word, they will slowly die from lack of attention.

If, on the other hand, our social training and choices have given us a hard heart that feels little or no guilt even when we are clearly disobeying God's commands, we must pull our behavior into line without the benefit of conscience. That may be hard to do when we know we could get by with it and not feel a thing, but it is a necessary step, and when we practice the right behavior long enough, we will begin to be tender again.

THE REALITY
OF GUILT

Feelings of guilt are one thing, but true guilt is quite another. It is possible to be very truly guilty in the sight of both God and man but feel nothing. And it is also possible to be declared free of guilt by the only Judge of the universe but still feel guilty inside. Our challenge is to find some way to manage both true guilt and false feelings of guilt. That should not be too difficult because there is only one solution for both problems. Jesus said it. "You shall know the truth, and the truth shall make you free" (John 8:32).

GETTING CLOSER
TO THE TRUTH

The reality of our true guilt often becomes more intense as we move closer to God. This is a frightening process for many Christians. They start out seeing part of their sin and ask God to cleanse them, then, five years into the Christian walk it seems that there is sin all over the place, at every corner. "What is the matter with me?" they cry. "I seem to be getting worse, not better!"

As we move closer to the light, the dirt shows more clearly. The seriousness of our past guilt can also look much worse as we learn to see our lives from God's perspective. The cruelty, selfishness, immoral sex, or lying that looked bad but not horrible when we were two days from it can haunt our conscience with an almost unbearable shame when we think of it three years down the road. This consciousness of sin and the internal guilt that such consciousness produces is in direct contrast to what we hoped the Christian life would be like.

We do not have to live with either the truth of guilt or the feelings of guilt. Jesus died to set us free from both.

New Testament writers often mentioned the fact that they were living with a completely clear conscience. The burden of past sins was totally gone, and they emotionally experienced what it was like to walk free of condemnation day after day. Read each of the following verses and make a few notes as to what each verse teaches you about a clean conscience. You will find my answers at the end of the chapter, but it will benefit you most to work your own answers before checking mine.

1. Hebrews 10:22

_____

_____

_____

2. Acts 23:1

_____

_____

_____

3. Acts 24:16

_____

_____

_____

4. 1 Timothy 3:9

_____

_____

_____

5. 1 Corinthians 8:1–13

_____

_____

_____

_____

_____

_____

This emotional freedom of a completely clean conscience was not something to be experienced only by super saints; it is part of your inheritance as a Christian. It was bought for you by Christ and is part of the "better covenant, which was established on better promises" (Heb. 8:6).

I sometimes hear Christians talk with longing for the days of Moses or Abraham or David or Solomon, but none of the promises made to the people of that time can compare with the promises made to us (Matt. 11:11). Many of these promises we inherit on this side of heaven, and one of those is the promise of achieving a life free of guilt (Heb. 9:14).

Achieving this life is not instantaneous, and it does not mean that we have lost the ability to sin. We will never lose that until we are in heaven. Temptation will be with us until then, but we can live without the guilt. We can feel clean inside.

The longest twelve inches in the world is the space between the head and the heart, but the key to living without guilt is to use our heads to train our hearts (conscience) in the truth. That task must be undertaken with skill and persistence. A lot of years and effort have gone into our conscience training thus far, and we should not expect the switch to be overnight, but it will come if we don't give up on the training.

Our first step is to determine the source of the feelings—the Holy Spirit, Satan, or social training—and go to work insisting that the body and mind accept only the truth. If the truth is that the Holy Spirit is convicting us, we need to control the body and stop the behavior. If the truth is that we are being falsely accused by Satan or our social training, call the feeling a lie. Just imagine that Satan is a delivery man ringing at your door with a package of guilt for you and refuse to sign. Don't even answer the door.

The second step is easy: Repeat step one. Then keep on

repeating again and again and again until the feelings finally give up and listen to reason.

THE TRUTH OF GUILT

The Christian worldview differs from the secular in that we accept that absolutes do exist. There is a real right and a real wrong that does not change with time and is not subject to the opinion of men. When these true and changeless standards are violated, we are guilty to the core.

It does not matter in the least whether we feel guilty or not. We *are* guilty just the same. God says so, and His word is final. But His word is also final if He says, "not guilty." Feelings are not supreme. God is.

The good news is that God has declared us innocent of our past sins. Our choices may have been bad in every sense of the word, and we may have intense feelings of shame and guilt over those choices, but when we repent, God proclaims something totally different from what our feelings say.

God can declare us clean because He has already paid our sin debt. We will study more about forgiveness and how it works in the next chapter, but for now, open your Bible and read Acts 10:9–22.

As a Jew, Peter had lived his entire life with an awareness of what was "clean" and what was "unclean." These words had nothing to do with dirt or even germs, but rather indicated a standard for acceptability. Those things that were "unclean" were defiled, unwanted, rejected by God, and to be avoided. In the Old Testament, God had specifically indicated many things that were to be considered "unclean."

But just as God has the right to declare something "unclean," He has the right to say that it is "clean"—worthy, acceptable, to be embraced—and that is what He did in Peter's dream.

At first, Peter kept arguing with God. God gave the command to eat, and Peter resisted obeying because the things he was told

Choice
207

to accept were "unclean." Finally, God challenged Peter, "Do not call anything impure that God has made clean" (Acts 10:15, NIV).

The same could be said for us and our guilt over past sins. Are we still calling "unclean" a self that God has declared to be pure? Do you believe your feelings or the truth of the judgment of God?

Below you will find an artist's conception of the sheet that was let down before Peter. Using a pencil, write on the sheet those choices you have made that created feelings of guilt. After you have written them all, pray to God, telling Him you intend to accept His view of these things, not your feelings. Then go back and erase all traces of those words until the sheet is clean.

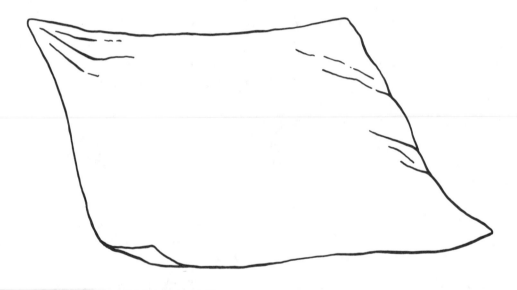

S U M M A T I O N

One thing I do know, both by personal experience and the assurance of God's Word, is that freedom from guilt is not only possible, it is normal for the growing Christian.

You should complete this chapter by filling in the personal summation page. Ask the hard questions. Don't be afraid to stretch and grow. God is not afraid of your questions. Face the issue of your real guilt and your feelings of guilt head-on with an honest heart. You won't remain in pain forever because His "better promise" is sure and part of that better promise is freedom from guilt.

 Personal Summation:

Personal Summation:

1. Drawing near to God gives us a heart full of assurance and free from a guilty conscience (Heb. 10:22).
2. Paul lived his life knowing he had fulfilled his duty to God and his conscience was clear (Acts 23:1).
3. Paul's clear conscience was something he worked for (Acts 24:16).
4. Being able to know that your conscience is clean is a requirement for serving as a deacon (1 Tim. 3:9).
5. We have an obligation to consider those personal acts that might encourage others to violate their weak consciences. It is better to choose not to exercise our freedom rather than create problems for a brother or sister in Christ (1 Cor. 8:1–13).
6. One of the reasons why the writer of Hebrews felt free to ask for the prayers of other people was because his conscience was clear (Heb. 13:18).

✣ CHAPTER 12

Forgiving Others, Forgiving Myself

I believe there is nothing that gives us better mental and spiritual health and more freedom than a thorough understanding of forgiveness. This rich topic is so broad, so powerful, so simple, and so complex that it could be a never-ending study like the study of love or God or redemption. Indeed, love, God, and redemption are all bathed in and almost defined by the concepts of forgiveness. Forgiveness is a resolution of the tension between grace and justice and a testimony of the triumph of love.

But forgiveness is also one of the most misunderstood concepts of life. I have been surprised at some of the comments mature Christians have made when I suggested that the resolution of their problems might be found in learning to forgive both others and themselves.

Below are ten statements about forgiveness. Mark each one either true or false.

1. Forgiveness means that you allow the person to do the same thing to you a second time.
   True   False

2. Forgiveness is saying that the offending person did not do wrong.
   True   False

3. Forgiveness requires us to pretend we like the offending party even if we feel angry.
   True   False

4. Forgiveness is a sign of weakness.
   True   False

5. Forgiveness will automatically repair the relationship between the offender and the offended.
   True   False

6. There is no relationship between our forgiving others and our ability to feel forgiven by God.
   True   False

7. If we forgive someone, they will never have to pay for their crime.
   True   False

8. If we forgive someone, we are saying that hurting us was OK.
   True   False

9. Forgiveness is the same as denying that we have been hurt.
   True   False

10. Forgiveness is something that only God can do.
    True   False

I have heard all of the above statements given as reasons to withhold forgiveness, but the truth is that all of the statements are false. You will find my responses to each statement at the end of the chapter.

WHAT FORGIVENESS IS NOT

Sometimes the easiest way to study what something is, is to study what the thing is not! When it comes to forgiveness, we find that it is not stupidity, it is not pretending, and it is not denial.

Forgiveness Is Not Stupidity

The person who told me the following story claimed it was true, and although it is hard to believe, I have run into enough similar situations in counseling that I suspect it just may be accurate.

It seems that a very bedraggled Christian woman was married for years to an abusive, practicing alcoholic. Finally she refused to allow herself to be abused and the children to be terrorized any longer. She changed the locks on the doors and insisted that her husband not come home until he made concrete progress toward recovery. She told him that she could forgive him for the past, but she would not allow the future to continue as it was.

A few weeks later he showed up at his wife's workplace and asked to borrow the car (he had totaled his own while drunk). At first she said no, but he began to badger her about her Christianity, saying that if she were really a Christian and had really forgiven him, she would forget the past and give him her keys. She gave in. He got drunk and totaled her car that same night.

The incredulous part of the story was that he came back to her a month later and asked to borrow the car *again*, this time for a job interview. He argued that they would never hire him if he showed up without a car and accused her by saying that she had obviously not been a big enough Christian to truly forgive; after all, didn't Jesus say we were to forgive seventy times seven? She gave him her keys, and he totaled her car for the second time.

Jesus told us that when we are dealing with dishonest people we should be as innocent as doves, but as shrewd as snakes (Matt. 10:16). We are never to cast our pearls of trust before swine (Matt. 7:6) because doing so puts us in danger.

Love and forgiveness do often involve elements of trust and risk. This is what Jesus meant when He said if someone slaps us on the right cheek we should offer him the other cheek also (Luke 6:29). But that risk does not involve making it easy for the other person to sin or ignoring our common sense. We do love our enemies and go an extra mile even with unkind people, but we never encourage another to sin by abusing our forgiveness.

Forgiveness Is Not Pretending

Too often we confuse forgiveness with a good feeling we are supposed to have inside. Not so. Forgiveness, like guilt, may involve our feelings, but it does not depend on feelings to exist.

We have only limited control over our feelings. We cannot turn them on and off like a water faucet. The human heart just doesn't feel on demand. Jesus gave us the command that we must forgive (Matt. 6:14), but if He were commanding that we feel something, He would have been asking the impossible.

Pain and loss always precede forgiveness. In fact, forgiveness cannot exist if there is no pain or loss. If we can wave our hand and truthfully say, "Oh, it doesn't matter," then there is no need for forgiveness. Because pain and loss are involved, other emotions are almost assumed. Anger, grief, struggle, resistance, hurt, and the need to fight can all be intermingled in the heart, and they may not instantly vanish just because the decision to forgive has been made.

Forgiveness is not identified by a feeling in the heart, but by a decision made with the head. When we forgive, we are simply making an agreement never to use the offense as a way to punish the offender. We don't try to get even. We don't try to restore our lost rights. We agree that the offender was wrong, but we also agree that we will allow God to handle the situation, not us.

Forgiveness Is Not Denial

Forgiveness is not denying we are hurt. There is only one thing that must exist before forgiveness can exist—pain. If there is no pain or loss, there can be no forgiveness.

If we are denying the pain, fighting against the pain, and refusing to allow ourselves to feel the full extent of the pain, we cannot forgive. We can only forgive to the degree that we can get in touch with the pain.

Sometimes in a session I will use my hands to demonstrate the difference between denial, human resistance to pain, and true forgiveness. For denial, the left hand is clenched into a fist. This represents the pain, hurt, or loss; the thing that needs to be forgiven. The right hand is turned around with the back of the hand toward the fist and the palm outward. The right hand is refusing to admit that the left fist exists. But the hurt does exist, and it won't go away simply because the right hand refuses to turn around and acknowledge its existence.

For human resistance to pain, the left fist and the right hand are in conflict. The fist is stationary, unmovable, resisting, while the right hand with the palm directed toward the fist and the fingers outstretched keeps banging into the fist. It continues to pound with the open palm. The fingers are stretched as though to run if they could and the right hand keeps backing off only to be drawn back and hit against the fist once more.

Forgiveness is altogether different. To demonstrate forgiveness, the tight left fist remains as unmovable as ever, only this time the right hand is more relaxed. The hand moves forward and the fingers wrap around the fist, embracing it. The right hand totally accepts the fist as reality and does not run. Then, after embracing, the right hand lets go. These two steps of embracing and letting go are the process of forgiveness. We cannot let go of something we refuse to embrace, and we cannot forgive something if we refuse to admit it exists. Denial makes forgiveness impossible.

How would you define forgiveness? Write a definition or give a brief illustration below.

———————————————————————————————

———————————————————————————————

———————————————————————————————

———————————————————————————————

My own definition is that forgiveness is a process that takes place when we have been hurt, then accept that hurt as part of our life and let the offending person, object, or situation go free. We set the offender free from our condemnation, free from our revenge, and free from any effort on our part to restore our lost rights.

AN ILLUSTRATION OF FORGIVENESS

If John Doe steals $200 from me and I agree before God to forgive John, I voluntarily accept the loss and agree never to use my knowledge of his guilt to hurt him or get even. I will lose the $200 whether I decide to forgive John or not. Forgiveness makes no difference in my loss. The only difference created by forgiveness is the difference between my bearing that loss in bitterness or bearing that loss in the freedom of forgiveness.

Forgiveness is not a matter between John and me, it is a matter between God and me. I agree to let John go and let God handle whatever happens next. Maybe I will get my money back, maybe I won't. Maybe John will be punished in this life for what he has done, maybe he won't. The relationship between John and me might be restored, but it might not. But whatever happens, it is God's job, not mine. That is forgiveness.

My decision to forgive John may involve feelings, but forgiveness can exist without them. Yet my feelings are important and they can cause me much pain. I need to deal with them and with

John. The feelings may come and go for quite some time after I have made the decision to forgive.

For example, let's assume that I felt pretty calm when I first made the decision to forgive John, but three months later I find that my kid needs braces and I can't buy them because John stole my money. I may find my emotions of hurt and anger coming back again. Does that mean I have not forgiven John? No. The decision to forgive was made. It means I have some emotional work to do by reminding myself of the decision again and again until my heart is in line with the truth that dealing with John is now up to God, not me. It is also up to God to provide what I need.

BUT IT'S NOT FAIR!

Forgiveness is hard because it conflicts with our sense of justice. Whether we are thinking about forgiving others or forgiving ourselves, something about the whole process seems so unfair. The guilty should pay. That is only right.

The Bible recognizes that there is nothing "fair" about forgiveness. Forgiveness is not fair, but it is right. To find out how this could be, work the following exercise.

Look up Ephesians 4:32; Colossians 3:13; 1 Peter 3:18; and Matthew 18:21–35. Below, explain why forgiveness is not "fair," but it is right.

_____

_____

_____

_____

_____

Forgiveness becomes right because of the reality of Calvary. Sin always demands a price. Someone must pay. But when forgiveness is active, it is not the offender who pays—it is the innocent. This substitution of debt becomes right because the innocent has volunteered to pay. Jesus volunteered to forgive us and pay our debt, and we have the privilege of volunteering to pay another's debt in response.

FORGIVENESS IS NOT RESOLUTION

We may find it hard to forgive because we assume that forgiveness and resolution are the same thing. They are not. Forgiveness does not necessarily provide instant resolution nor will it guarantee reconciliation in a relationship.

If John steals my $200 and I forgive John, that does not mean that I like John, or that John and I become friends again, or that all my emotions are peaceful. I am guaranteed that there will be an emotional resolution inside me that will follow my forgiveness; Jesus said I will have peace of heart (John 16:33), and He promised that as I grow to love Him, He will give me more love for others (Rom. 5:5; John 15:5; Gal. 5:22; 1 John 4:16–17). He will give me a new heart when my own heart is cold and unresponsive (Ezek. 36:26). The peace and love may not come instantly, but they will come.

The resolution of the situation between John and me is an entirely different matter. We have no scriptural guarantee for that. One reason is because it does not depend on me alone. I may forgive John completely and even feel the freedom of that forgiveness, but before our relationship can be restored, John must know I have forgiven him and he must accept my forgiveness.

If John leaves and never hears of my decision to accept the loss as my own and let him go free, then as far as John is concerned, the relationship between us is the same as if my forgiveness did not exist.

Our relationship will also not be restored if John knows about

my forgiveness but insists that he really does not owe me anything. He cannot accept my forgiveness unless he admits that he
owes me a debt.

Forgiveness stops my suffering and makes my heart right with
God, but it does not necessarily end the struggle John has with
me because that resolution depends partly on John.

Using the illustration of resolving the relationship between John
Doe and myself as a guide, think of how these principles reflect
the resolution of the relationship between ourselves and God.
Write a few sentences about how the resolution of both situations involves forgiveness. You might want to read John 3:1–18
before you begin.

FORGIVENESS
AND GUILT

The longer I am in practice, the greater impact a simple
statement of Jesus in Matthew 7:1–2 has on my thinking and my
counsel. He said, "Judge not, that you be not judged. For with
what judgment you judge, you will be judged; and with the
measure you use, it will be measured back to you."

When a client complains of feeling controlled and manipulated, I try to see how controlling and manipulative she may be.
When someone feels rejected, I look to see how well he is
accepting those who are already in his life. If he feels the
church is cold and critical, I try to determine how critical and
unresponsive he is. And if someone is struggling with continual
feelings of guilt, I look for someone they have not fully forgiven.

This formula does not always work; Jesus experienced a rejection, but it was not due to His rejection of others. Still if I have a

client who is filled with feelings of rejection, it is a good bet that the person is receiving the same measure back to herself as she is giving to others.

In similar fashion, there appears to be a strong relationship between our ability to feel forgiven by God and our willingness to forgive others. Feelings of guilt and an unforgiving heart often go hand in hand. If we want to stop feeling guilty, we will have to forgive others.

Sometimes we have not been able to forgive because we have not been willing to get in touch with our pain. We can't let go until we embrace. At other times, we may be stuck in the pain and unwilling to let go.

LETTING GO

Our God-given imagination can be a strong source for either good or evil. One of the good ways it can be used is to get us emotionally in touch with something we have been unable to fully process with our intellect. We saw an example of this in Chapter 9, when we sat in God's lap and looked at the earth (see exercise p. 160).

The following story may help you get emotionally in touch with the process of forgiveness in your own life. The story is true.

One of the things I like best about private practice counseling with a ministry is the unbelievable variety of people with whom I work. I may deal with a young mother trying to get her baby to sleep through the night, a couple very much in love who are going through our premarital counseling, and a suicidal drug addict—all in the same evening. But in all my counseling practice, I have never run into someone like Trudy.

I had been seeing Trudy (not her real name) for several months. She was in her thirties and had been a prostitute and drug runner with heavy occult involvement since she was a child.

Trudy's conversion to Christianity did not occur in storybook fashion. She struggled tremendously, dropping in and out of the old life-style and constantly battling suicidal thoughts and depression. And to complicate matters even more, when she did take a limited stand as a Christian, she was attacked from all sides. When she refused to make a drug run for her pimp, he retaliated by having her gang-raped by six men.

She sat in my office the next day, bruised and hard as stone. She figured she had two choices. She could either put a contract on the lives of the men involved, or she could replace the gun I had convinced her to sell and do the job herself. I had no doubt that she was perfectly able to carry through with either plan.

When I suggested that there might be a third choice, she listened closely but was as cautious as a cornered bear. It took about half an hour as I explained about forgiveness and the idea of letting Jesus administer justice in the matter.

Trudy thought for a moment, then said no with a firmness and resolve. "Why, not?" I asked. "Because Jesus might be too nice to them," she truthfully replied.

I couldn't argue with that logic. Jesus is all grace and no one, not Trudy nor her persecutors, is beyond His love. But she slowly began to see that she might consider this third course of action for her own sake, not for the sake of her enemy. As long as she held the pursuit of justice in her hands, her enemies were not free, but neither was she.

At last she agreed that the third choice might be best, but I could tell that the decision was only head deep. She still was not connecting emotionally.

I asked Trudy to relax and close her eyes and visualize each of the six men standing next to her along the wall. We talked about each and what she could remember about them. She described the physical look of each. For some she had first names; one we could identify only by the boots he wore. As we talked, her face became troubled and after a few moments she opened her eyes long enough to glance to the right. The images in her mind were becoming strong enough that she was touching the "reality" of the men beside her and needed to make sure it was only her imagination.

Once the men were "real" enough to have emotional connection, I told her that I had invited someone else to join us. Jesus had come, and He was waiting outside the door. I asked her permission to let Him into the room and once she gave it, I got up and opened and closed the door. Jesus was now "standing" to her left.

We talked for a moment about what she believed Jesus looked like, then I said, "There are holding cells outside the door. Six of them. They are very strong and Jesus has the keys. He would like to take each of the men and put each one in a cell, but He will not do so without your permission. You can either keep justice in your own hands, or you can give it to Him. The choice is yours. I cannot tell you what Jesus will do with the men. You are right in saying that He is kind. He has been kind to you. But He is also just. One may get AIDS next week and die a slow, agonizing death that would be worse than a bullet from you. One may ask forgiveness and turn his life around and live a long time with a wife and family. Another may not be brought to justice until after he dies. I don't know what Jesus will do with each man. But I can tell you that He will be fair. Will you let Jesus take one of the men?"

It had been hard enough for Trudy to connect on an intellectual level with the idea of forgiving and turning the pursuit of justice over to God, but now that it had become emotionally real, she struggled in her chair and her eyes almost began to softly tear (Trudy never cried).

"Will you let Jesus take one?" I repeated.

"Only one."

"Which one do you want Him to take?" I asked.

Trudy described the man, and I asked her to "see" Jesus reach in front of her and take the man by the hand. Just before they left the room, I asked her to look at the man's face as he turned back toward her. He pulled, but Jesus was stronger and would not let go. I opened and closed the door for a second time, and "Boots" was out of the room.

Slowly we worked through the remaining five men. The last was her long-time pimp and occult leader. All she wanted was to have him dead. Releasing him to Jesus to suffer a fate over which she had no control was very hard for Trudy, but at last she did and the room was empty. All the visions had gone.

Trudy looked up and smiled. "I don't understand," she said, "but I feel a lot better." I understood. When we forgive others, we gain the most freedom.

If you have been through a situation where you have completed step one of forgiveness (feeling the pain), but are having trouble with step two (letting go), you might consider walking through an imagination exercise such as the one Trudy and I went through that day.

If you are having trouble forgiving yourself, imagine that part of yourself as a separate entity. If you can, remember the age you were at the time, how you looked, what you might have worn. Anything that will help you get more emotionally in touch with the reality of yourself at that time will be helpful.

Just as you might imagine Jesus taking away a person who had offended you, let Him take that part of yourself under His control and justice. He will be both loving and fair (something you can never be) because He is all knowing, but you are not.

WHY WE SHOULD FORGIVE

We should forgive because Jesus commanded us to do it (Matt. 6:14). Forgiving others is a debt that we owe God because He has forgiven us. Our own ability to feel forgiven by God is strongly connected to our willingness to forgive others (and self). Even the familiar Lord's Prayer says, "Forgive us our debts, / As we forgive our debtors" (Matt. 6:12).

In the book of Ephesians, Paul tells us, "Be kind to one another, tenderhearted, forgiving one another, just as God in Christ forgave you" (Eph. 4:32). And lest we miss the point he repeats in Colossians, "Therefore, as the elect of God, holy and beloved, put on tender mercies, kindness, humility, meekness, longsuffering; bearing with one another, and forgiving one another, if anyone has a complaint against another; even as Christ forgave you, so you also must do" (Col. 3:12–13).

We love because He first loved us (1 John 4:10–11,19), and we forgive because we have experienced the forgiveness of Christ.

But there is another reason we should forgive, a purely self-centered reason: Forgiveness sets us free.

In Matthew 18, Jesus tells the parable of the unmerciful servant. He says that a king had a servant who owed him a vast amount of money. When the servant was unable to pay and begged the king to give him more time, the king was gracious and granted even more than the servant requested; he completely forgave the debt.

However, the story doesn't end there. That servant went out and found a fellow servant who only owed him a few dollars. When his fellow servant could not pay, he had him thrown in prison. When the king heard about the situation, he called the unmerciful servant into his presence a second time.

"You wicked servant!" said the king. "I forgave you all that debt because you begged me. Should you not also have had compassion on your fellow servant, just as I had pity on you?" Then the king turned to the jailer and commanded that the unmerciful servant be kept in the jailer's care until the debt was paid.

Jesus makes a very unusual statement when he finishes telling this story. He says, "So My heavenly Father also will do to you if each of you, from his heart, does not forgive his brother his trespasses."

Since we have no physical jailers here on earth to take us away when we fail to forgive, have you ever wondered what jailers Jesus was talking about? In the King James Version the word *tormentors* is used instead of *jailers*. Young's Analytical Concordance to the Bible interprets the word as "one who tries, or tests, an inquisitor." It conveys the idea of a man being turned over to someone who will punish until the truth comes out.

The tormentors who try us until the truth comes out are the

twin worms of guilt and bitterness. They bind us in prison and punish until we admit the truth of our unrighteousness and that we have no right to demand another pay a debt when we cannot pay our own.

Getting rid of the worms is a mighty good reason to forgive.

SUMMATION

Finish this chapter by filling in the personal summation page. If you have others you have not forgiven, you might consider making a list and writing, "Lord I forgive _____ for _____." After you have listed the names and forgiven each thing they have done against you, write the date that you made the decision to forgive.

You may also want to work through the same process as you forgive yourself, and perhaps do the imagery in the exercise on page 222.

Personal Summation:

ANSWER KEY

The following are the answers for the exercise on page 212.

1. Forgiveness can involve the risk of someone hurting us again, but it is not a sure thing that we voluntarily allow when we have a choice in the matter.

2. The very nature of forgiveness is that we admit the other person did wrong. If there is no wrong, there can be no forgiveness.

3. We never have to lie or pretend about our feelings.

4. It takes phenomenal strength to forgive.

5. There is a difference between forgiveness and resolution. One does not necessarily preclude the other.

6. We cannot feel forgiven by God if we will not forgive others (Matt. 18:21–35).

7. When we forgive, we turn the punishment over to God. He is just.

8. Hurting us is a sin just like hurting anyone else. We never say that sin is OK.

9. We must admit to and embrace the pain of being hurt before we can forgive. You can never let go until you first embrace.

10. Because forgiveness is something God commands us to do, we can do what He says even though emotional resolution is a work of the Spirit that may follow later.

PART FIVE

Seeing Myself Through God's Eyes

CHAPTER 13 ❧

The Truth about Self

Imagine that you are a poor orphan who grew up going from foster home to foster home and scratched for a limited education. Then as a young adult you are employed in a fish cannery, working on the line. One day you are called into the front office to find a man in a business suit waiting for you with briefcase in hand. He informs you that you are the long-lost child of a multimillionaire. Your father has been looking for you for twenty years, and you are heir to everything he owns.

The truth is that you have always had enough money to buy the cannery and three more besides if you wanted them, but you did not know the truth about yourself, so your actions over the years had been consistent with what you *thought* you were, not with the truth. Hollywood stories and paperback novels are made of dreams such as this, but in the real world these things never happen. Or do they?

Thousands of Christians have experiences similar to that of our cannery worker millionaire when they come to realize the truth of what they are in Christ and they stopped believing themselves to be poor, weak, and abandoned. While this experience seldom makes a difference in your bank account, it makes all the difference in your self-esteem, confidence, joy, and peace. And when you think about it—without confidence, joy, and peace, money isn't worth much.

POSITIVE
AFFIRMATION

For many years secular self-help groups and professional counselors have tried to help people by giving them "positive affirmations." These statements are pasted on mirrors or carried in wallets. They are memorized, meditated on, and/or repeated over and over all day in an effort to drive the statement deep into the mind and heart. That can be an effective process, but I have had a problem with some of the statements that my clients have been encouraged to use. Statements like I am good, I am worthy, and I deserve the best in life may make someone feel better for a short while, but I wonder about their long-term good because statements like these are lies.

I never could see the value of substituting a set of lies that sound bad for a set of lies that sound good. Lies are still lies no matter how you cut them.

The truth is that we are not good, but we are loved. We are not worthy, but we are chosen. We do not deserve the best, but we have been given the best of heaven.

In an effort to solve this problem, one day I called a friend who has been a Bible teacher for many years and asked her to bring her Bible to my office for a joint project. We spent a couple of hours going through our personal Bibles, looking at the verses that we had marked over a period of years, discussing why they meant so much to us.

I typed out many of the verses, paraphrasing them in whatever way seemed appropriate. Then I put blanks where the pronouns or names were in the original text. What remained was a list of statements that were not really quotes from the Bible, but they were based on specific scriptures. I read the list out loud, substituting my name for each blank. The process blessed me so much that I made copies of the list. Since that time many others have used the list to give themselves *true* positive affirmations, not lies.

The next several pages contain the true positive statements just discussed. Read through the list slowly and fill in each blank with your name. After you have been through the list once, you may decide to record the statements. There are enough to make about a thirty-minute cassette tape. Then, when you are driving, going to sleep, or jogging, play the tape and listen to your own voice saying true things about you and your relationship with God.

_____ will sing of God's strength in the morning. She will sing of God's love because God is _____'s fortress; God is _____'s refuge in times of trouble (see Ps. 59:16).

_____ waited patiently for the Lord. The Lord turned to _____ and heard her cry. The Lord lifted _____ up out of a slimy pit and out of the mud and mire. The Lord sat _____'s feet on a rock and gave her a firm place to stand (see Ps. 40:1–3).

Although _____'s sins are like scarlet, these sins shall be as white as snow. Even if they are red like crimson, _____'s sins shall be like wool (see Isa. 1:18).

Jesus will thoroughly purge away _____'s sins and dross. Jesus will remove all of _____'s impurities (see Isa. 1:25).

_____, do not call to your mind the former things; do not dwell on the past. See, Jesus is doing a new thing in your life (see Isa. 43:18–19).

Jesus has armed _____ with strength for battle. He has made her enemies fall at _____'s feet (see 2 Sam. 22:40).

Jesus has exalted _____ above those who rise up against her. He rescues _____ from the violent man (see 2 Sam. 22:49).

God will keep _____ in perfect peace, because _____'s mind is steadfast toward God and because _____ trusts in God (see Isa. 26:3).

The Lord is _____'s shepherd, _____ shall lack nothing. Jesus makes _____ to lie down in green pastures, and he leads _____ beside quiet waters. Jesus restores _____'s soul. He guides _____ in the paths of righteousness for His name's sake. Even though _____ walks through the valley of the shadow of death, _____ will fear no evil because God is with _____. God's rod and God's staff are a comfort to _____. God prepares a table before _____ in the presence of her enemies. God anoints _____'s head with oil. _____'s cup overflows. Surely goodness and love will follow _____ all the days of her life, and _____ will dwell in the house of the Lord forever (see Ps. 23).

Can a mother forget the baby at her breast and have no compassion on the child she has borne? Yes, sometimes a mother may forget, but God will never forget _____ (see Isa. 49:15).

When _____ hopes in God, she will not be disappointed (see Isa. 49:23).

God knows the plans that He has for _____. They are plans to prosper her and not to harm her. These plans will give _____ a future and a hope (see Jer. 29:11).

_____ will seek God and will find God because _____ searches for God with all her heart (see Jer. 29:13).

Do not be afraid, _____. Since the first day that you set your mind to gain understanding and to humble yourself before God, your words were heard by Him (see Dan. 10:12).

God Himself will search for _____ and look after her. As a shepherd looks after His scattered flock when He is with them, so God will look after _____ (see Ezek. 34:11–12).

Jesus will give _____ a new heart and put a new spirit in _____. Jesus will take from _____ that heart of stone and will give _____ a heart of flesh (see Ezek. 36:26).

This is the word of the Lord to _____: It will not be by might that the deed is accomplished; it will not be by power. The thing that will make a difference and accomplish the task will be the Spirit of the Lord (see Zech. 4:6).

Because Jesus sets _____ free; _____ shall be totally free indeed (see John 8:36).

Jesus left peace with _____. His own peace He has given to her (see John 14:27).

But God demonstrated His love for _____ in this way: while _____ was still a sinner, Christ died for _____ (see Rom. 5:8).

_____ is not condemned in any way because _____ is in Christ Jesus (see Rom. 8:1).

_____ is not controlled by the sinful nature but by the Spirit because the Spirit of God lives in _____ (see Rom. 8:9).

For _____ did not receive a spirit that makes her a slave again to fear, but _____ received the spirit of adoption by which _____ has the right to call God, "Abba, Father" (see Rom. 8:15).

_____ is convinced that neither death nor life, neither angels nor demons, neither height nor depth, nor anything else in all creation will be able to separate _____ from the love of God that is in Christ Jesus (see Rom. 8:38–39).

_____ can cast all her cares on Jesus, because Jesus cares about _____ (see 1 Peter 5:7).

Could it be that _____ does not know? Has _____ never heard? The Lord is the everlasting God, the Creator of the ends of the earth. God will not grow tired or weary. His understanding is so deep no one can know it all. God gives strength to the weary and increases the power of the weak. Even the youths grow tired and weary and athletes sometimes stumble and fall, but this will not be true for _____ because she waits on the Lord, and those who wait on the Lord will renew their strength. They will mount up with wings as eagles; they will run and not grow weary, they will walk and not be faint (see Isa. 40:28–31).

The eyes of the Lord are on _____, and His ears are open to _____'s cry (see Ps. 34:15).

OUR TRUE SELF

We have spent the last twelve chapters going back through our life, looking at pieces of self that we have cast off along the way. We have examined what we know, what we remember, what we feel, and what our emotional reaction is to what we see. All of this has been part of our truth.

But there is more truth than what we see and remember. There are the things concerning us that God says are true. We may not always feel this truth. Our limited view of our daily world may encourage us to doubt the truth. But God says it is real, and we may often find ourselves at the crossroads, caught between believing our feelings and believing our Lord.

Three things the Lord says are true of His children: We are significant, we have been accepted by Him, and we are secure both in this world and the next. If we could believe that—really believe it—what a difference it would make in our ability to accept ourselves! Yet, it is difficult for us to believe these things when we look at those events of our past and present that make us feel worthless, rejected, and insecure.

In order to completely accept ourselves, we need to believe what God says about us more strongly than we believe the pain that makes us reject those things about self we do not like. Dr. Neil T. Anderson has helped many people choose the right fork in the road. He has also written an excellent booklet, *Steps to Freedom in Christ,* that I often use in counseling. On the last two pages of that booklet, Dr. Anderson lists scriptures which demonstrate the truth of our significance, our acceptability, and our security in Christ.

There is enough truth and power in these statements and references to provide a hundred Bible study courses. One statement, thoroughly understood and applied, can make a lifelong difference in how we think of ourselves.

I would encourage you to go through each of the three sections slowly, letting the full impact of what is being said hit you at not only an intellectual level but on an emotional level as well.

I am significant because....
I am the salt of the earth (Matt. 5:13).
I am the light of the world (Matt. 5:14).
I am God's child (John 1:12; 1 John 3:1–3).
I am a branch of the true vine, a channel of His life (John 15:1,5).
I have been chosen and appointed to bear fruit (John 15:16).
I am a personal witness of Christ's (Acts 1:8).
I am God's temple (1 Cor. 3:16).
I am a member of Christ's body (1 Cor. 12:27).
I am God's coworker (1 Cor. 3:9; 2 Cor. 6:1).
I am a saint (Eph. 1:1).
I have been raised up and I am seated with Christ (Eph. 2:6).

I am God's workmanship (Eph. 2:10).

I am a citizen of heaven (Eph. 2:6; Phil. 3:20).

I am acceptable because ...

I am Christ's friend (John 15:15).

I have been justified (Rom. 5:1).

I am joined to the Lord, and I am one spirit with Him (1 Cor. 6:17).

I am a member of Christ's body (1 Cor. 12:27).

I have been made righteous (2 Cor. 5:21).

I have been adopted as God's child (Eph. 1:5).

I have direct access to God through the Holy Spirit (Eph. 2:18).

I am of God's household (Eph. 2:19).

I am a fellow citizen with the rest of the saints (Eph. 2:19).

I may approach God with boldness and confidence (Eph. 3:12).

I have been redeemed and forgiven of all my sins (Col. 1:14).

I am complete in Christ (Col. 2:10).

I am secure because. . . .

I am a child of God (John 1:12; Gal. 3:26–28).

I am assured that all things work together for good (Rom. 8:28).

I cannot be separated from the love of God (Rom. 8:35).

I am free from any condemning charges against me (Rom. 8:1).

I have been established, anointed, and sealed by God (2 Cor. 1:21–22).

I have been given the Holy Spirit as a pledge, guaranteeing my inheritance to come (Eph. 1:13–14).

I have been delivered from the domain of darkness and transferred to the kingdom of Christ (Col. 1:13).

I am hidden with Christ in God (Col. 3:3).

I am confident that the good work that God has begun in me will be completed (Phil. 1:6).

I can do all things through Him who strengthens me (Phil. 4:13).

I have not been given a spirit of fear, but of power, love, and a sound mind (2 Tim. 1:7).

I can find grace and mercy in time of need (Heb. 4:16).

I am born of God, and the evil one cannot touch me (1 John 5:18).

WHAT HAPPENED TO ME?

We sometimes have trouble believing that we are significant, accepted, and secure because we do not have a clear knowledge of the significance of Calvary. Those few hours when the Son of God volunteered to pay the price for my sin and your sin were indeed the turning point of history and eternity.

When I agree with God that I owe Him a debt which I cannot pay and I accept His forgiveness and Jesus' payment for my sin, I go through the experience that is sometimes called "salvation" or being "born again" or "conversion." I may feel a lot at that moment, or I may feel very little, but the truth is that many fantastic things happen to me instantly and I will never be the same again.

Just a few of these things are listed below. Read through them slowly and look up the references. Let yourself become thoroughly familiar with what your moment of change looked like from heaven's viewpoint and what happened in truth when you were accepted into the family of God.

Because of Calvary....

I have been justified, completely forgiven, and made righteous (Rom. 5:1).

I died with Christ and died to the power of sin's rule in my life (Rom. 6:1–6).

I have been bought with a price. I am not my own. I belong to God (1 Cor. 6:19–20).

I have been made righteous (2 Cor. 5:21).

I have been chosen in Christ before the foundation of the world to be holy and without blame before Him (Eph. 1:4).

I have direct access to God through the Spirit (Eph. 2:18).

I have been delivered (rescued) from the domain of darkness (Satan's rule) and transferred to the kingdom of Christ (Col. 1:13).

I have been redeemed and forgiven of all my sins, the debt against me has been canceled (Col. 1:14; 2:13–14).

I have been made complete in Christ (Col. 2:10).

I have been given the spirit of power, love, and self-discipline (2 Tim. 1:7).

I have been saved and called (set apart) according to God's doing (2 Tim. 1:9).

I have been given exceedingly great and precious promises by God by which I am partaker of the divine (God's) nature (2 Peter 1:4).

SUMMATION

Complete this chapter by filling in the personal summation page. You may want to write about your own experiences with God, or take note of questions that have come up as you studied through the many Scripture references in this chapter.

Personal Summation:

PART
SIX

Accepting
Myself

CHAPTER 14 ✣

Answering the Question of Who I Am

We started off this guidebook by asking the simple question, Dear God, Who Am I? and you have spent these last many pages searching for the reply. Every exercise you have completed, every memory you have recorded, and every statement that hit home when you read it has gone into forming the unique answer that is for you and you alone.

Now go back and review all you have done. What did you discover about your genetic heritage? Where do you fit in the family? In God's eternal scheme? How did your environment shape and form you? What did you record about your history in Chapter 8? Have you found it hard to accept the wrong choices you have made? How did they change your life? What about the wrong choices of others? Have you forgiven others and yourself?

Go back over the personal summations one more time. These are statements reflecting who you are. What do they say about you?

There is one more personal summation page to fill in. This one is purposely lined to keep you brief and organized. Put more thought into this page than you did the others. Begin with the phrase, *I am . . .* and continue on from there stating the significant things about who you are.

Personal Summation:

I am

There is one last item before you leave this guidebook. Following this explanation, you will find a certificate and a song. The certificate is to commemorate the day you not only answered the question Who am I? but agreed to accept the answer that came back.

Remember, there is a difference between acceptance and approval. We can accept ourselves without necessarily approving of all we have done or all the things that have been done to us. The very fact that we forgive both ourselves and others indicates that there has been wrong and pain and things that neither God nor we approve of. Acceptance is different.

When we accept ourselves, we are agreeing to embrace all we know of self as our own. We voluntarily reach out, give it a hug, and welcome it home, trusting God to take care of the less than desirable parts.

Now read the last page, and prayerfully fill it in.

WELCOME HOME

To the praise of the glory of his grace, wherein he hath made us accepted in the beloved

Ephesians 1:6

Because I am thoroughly accepted by God

Because God is and has been in control of my life

Because I want to embrace all God gives me

Because God holds the final justice of all things

I, _____ ,
in this day of the _____ in the month of _____ ,
in the year of our Lord _____ ,
do hereby let it be known that I am embracing as my own all that
God has given to me genetically, all that He has placed
in my environment, and all the choice that both others and
myself have made that have shaped me into who I am today.
With a grateful heart and much expectation I believe,
"He which hath begun a good work in (me) will perform
it until the day of Jesus Christ"

Philippians 1:6.

We Have Been Accepted

Chris K. Wommack

We have been ac - cep - ted by the Lord Most High We
I have been ac - cep - ted by the Lord Most High I

have been ac - cep - ted by the Lord Most High so let us
have been ac - cep - ted by the Lord Most High so I'll ac -

learn to ac - cept one a - noth - er in Christ for
cept all I am and with joy I will cry. *O

we have been ac - cep - ted by the Lord
I have been ac - cep - ted by the Lord